TO

FROM

CHASE THE FUN

Books by Annie F. Downs

CHASE THE FUN

100 DAYS TO DISCOVER FUN RIGHT WHERE YOU ARE

ANNIE F. DOWNS

NEW YORK TIMES BESTSELLING AUTHOR

Revell

a division of Baker Publishing Group
Grand Rapids, Michigan

© 2022 by Annie F. Downs

Published by Revell
a division of Baker Publishing Group
PO Box 6287, Grand Rapids, MI 49516-6287
www.revellbooks.com

Printed in Canada

Library of Congress Cataloging-in-Publication Data
Names: Downs, Annie F., 1980– author.
Title: Chase the fun : 100 days to discover fun right where you are / Annie F. Downs.
Description: Grand Rapids, MI : Revell, a division of Baker Publishing Group, [2022]
Identifiers: LCCN 2021045519 | ISBN 9780800738761 (cloth) | ISBN 9781493436255 (ebook)
Subjects: LCSH: Play—Religious aspects—Christianity—Miscellanea. | Recreation—Religious
    aspects—Christianity—Miscellanea. | Laughter—Religious aspects—Christianity—Miscellanea. |
    Amusements—Religious aspects—Christianity—Miscellanea.
Classification: LCC BT709 .D69 2021 | DDC 233/.5—dc23
LC record available at https://lccn.loc.gov/2021045519

Unless otherwise indicated, Scripture quotations are from THE HOLY BIBLE, NEW INTERNATIONAL VERSION®, NIV® Copyright © 1973, 1978, 1984, 2011 by Biblica, Inc.® Used by permission. All rights reserved worldwide.

Scripture quotations labeled ESV are from The Holy Bible, English Standard Version® (ESV®), copyright © 2001 by Crossway, a publishing ministry of Good News Publishers. Used by permission. All rights reserved. ESV Text Edition: 2016

Scripture quotations labeled MSG are from THE MESSAGE, copyright © 1993, 2002, 2018 by Eugene H. Peterson. Used by permission of NavPress. All rights reserved. Represented by Tyndale House Publishers, Inc.

Scripture quotations labeled NASB are from the (NASB®) New American Standard Bible®, Copyright © 1960, 1971, 1977, 1995, 2020 by The Lockman Foundation. Used by permission. All rights reserved. www.lockman.org

Scripture quotations labeled NLT are from the Holy Bible, New Living Translation, copyright © 1996, 2004, 2007, 2013, 2015 by Tyndale House Foundation. Used by permission of Tyndale House Publishers, Inc., Carol Stream, Illinois 60188. All rights reserved.

Scripture quotations labeled TLB are from The Living Bible, copyright © 1971. Used by permission of Tyndale House Publishers, Inc., Carol Stream, Illinois 60188. All rights reserved.

Portions of this text have been taken from That Sounds Fun published by Revell, 2021.

The author is represented by Alive Literary Agency, www.aliveliterary.com.

Baker Publishing Group publications use paper produced from sustainable forestry practices and post-consumer waste whenever possible.

Interior design by William Overbeeke.

22   23   24   25   26   27   28   7   6   5   4   3   2   1

TO EMILY P. FREEMAN—

for all the ways your constant and faithful friendship
invites me back to myself.
Thank you for teaching me how to chase the fun.

(And to Shannan and Amber—
may we always rally for each other.)

Throughout this devotional, you will see questions about fun that my friends have asked me on social media, via email, and at events across the country. We include them here to remind you that you aren't alone in what you wonder.

CONTENTS

Where do I start? | Ashlie

How do I find the time? | Jana

How do I shut off the part of my brain that says productivity > fun? | Emily

How do I find the energy for fun? | Denise

How do I prioritize fun? | Anonymous Friend

Where do you even start imagining what fun might be for you? | Anonymous Friend

How do I discover new hobbies without spending a million dollars or being wasteful? | Erin

I've tried/given up many hobbies. How do I change the failure narrative and find one I like? | Anonymous Friend

START HERE

Chase the Fun

And let us run with perseverance the race marked out for us.

HEBREWS 12:1

A few years ago, I was texting with my friend Emily P. Freeman, another author and podcaster and one of my favorite spiritual directors, and we were talking about our work. Emily specializes in helping people make decisions. "What is the next right thing?" That's the question she poses to her readers and fans (like me) on a weekly basis through her podcast and in her book.

I don't remember the conversation as clearly as Emily does, but we had a talk about what we wanted to do next. What type of work, what type of creative things, how we wanted to spend our time. And as Emily tells it, as we were processing what to do next, I said to her, "Well, just chase the fun!"

Chase the fun.

It's a thing we did when we were kids. It was our first instinct—to chase the fun. It was our top priority, biggest goal, most important motivator. But that's not the case anymore, is it? Being an adult, whether you are twenty, forty, sixty, or eighty-five, is different than when you were a kid. We used to play, we used to run and jump and dance and swing and slide and skin up our knees. We used to chase the fun.

While there are parts of childhood that are best left there—like the skinned knees, thank you very much—there is something important that we lost when we stopped chasing the fun. It doesn't mean every day is a party, and it doesn't mean we run from our responsibilities. But I just wonder if you picked up this book because it feels like something is missing in your life and you're trying to find it again. So, what would it look like for you to pay a little closer attention to the life you already have and the world in which you already live, and give a little chase to the fun that is right in front of you?

CHASE THE FUN

What was one of your favorite things to do as a kid?

Does Fun Really Matter?

No one looks stupid when they're having fun.
AMY POEHLER

This question comes up a lot in conversations around me: *Does fun really matter?* It isn't often asked quite that directly, but more in ways that bob and weave around the question. In our lives today, with the schedules we keep and the calendars we fill, we only have space for what REALLY matters. I do not have time in my life, and I bet you don't either, for things that are without some level of purpose. And I'm not sure we are meant to. I believe God made us each on purpose with a purpose, and our days are not meant to be wasted.

So when it comes to how we fill our calendars and our lives, we insist—and rightly so—on filling our lives with what matters. Unfortunately, fun often falls into the category of things to fill in the gaps when all the important things have been prioritized and scheduled.

I believe we make time for everything that makes us feel healthy. For you, that could be a trip to the grocery store or a walk around your neighborhood, an appointment with a counselor or an evening with your small group from church. The things that shape you into who you want to be are the things that get a spot on your calendar. That's true for me too.

A truth I keep experiencing is that I am my healthiest self when the activities and opportunities I prioritize on my calendar include things that are fun to me. Fun isn't frivolous or unnecessary. It isn't wasteful or useless. What fun unlocks in your heart and mind and soul—whether it's a day of fun or a half hour of fun—is incredibly important. (It's why we need hobbies . . . stick around and I'll help you find one or two!) Fun matters because it is a puzzle piece in the bigger picture that's shaping each of us into the healthiest version of ourselves.

CHASE THE FUN

What other things (besides fun) do you prioritize on your calendar to live a healthy life?

Is Fun a Spiritual Thing?

> In commanding us to glorify Him, God is inviting us to enjoy Him.
>
> C. S. LEWIS

Isn't everything we do spiritual?

Whether it's chopping an onion or driving in the carpool or doing brain surgery or playing a game of tennis, can't it all be spiritual? It seems to be less about what we do and more about why we do it and what is going on in our minds while we are doing it. It is all spiritual; it is all about more than what we can see with our eyes.

In her book *Walking on Water*, Madeleine L'Engle writes about how all art is sacred because we are always turning chaos into cosmos when we create. I find that true in every area of my life. If I am out on a jog, listening to a podcast that tells me something new about God, and then it causes me to think and change and pray and wonder, that run has become spiritual. If I am making a soup, chopping and stirring and thinking through why it matters to feed people I love, that soup making has become spiritual. If I am sitting around a table with my best friends as we discuss heartbreak and deep joy, our conversation is about more than just what is going on with us. It's about how God is at work in our lives, and that dinner has become spiritual.

Fun is the same. Whether you are screaming on a roller coaster or putting a puzzle together in the dining room of your house, it can be spiritual. All it takes for an activity to go spiritual is if you ask your heart questions as you do it. If you struggle through a puzzle and find yourself overly frustrated, ask yourself why and keep chasing down that rabbit trail. If you are riding down the road listening to your favorite music with the windows rolled down, ask yourself why it feels so fun and restful. The answer will be spiritual.

CHASE THE FUN

Look for the ways that the ordinary parts of your day today—breakfast, a walk, a conversation with a friend—can be spiritual.

Why Did I Quit Having Fun?

> We don't stop playing because we grow old; we grow old because we stop playing.
>
> GEORGE BERNARD SHAW

This is the question we need to answer. But the question that comes to my mind first is "WHEN did I quit having fun?" Scroll back in your mind the way you can scroll back through pictures on your phone, and think back to when you had fun on a regular basis.

Was it before your parents divorced?

Was it before a grandparent passed away?

Was it before you graduated high school?

Was it before that traumatic experience?

Was it before that stressful season?

Was it before you grew up?

Finding the WHEN will help you answer the WHY. And both questions are important. Knowing your history helps you shape your present and your future. If we believe fun matters and can be a spiritual thing, we need to find it again. And to find the heart behind the fun, we have to go back and figure out where we left it. It's not that we can pick back up right where we left off. Sadly, that's not an option. But seeing that place, seeing that moment, acknowledging the pain or stress or sadness or worry that happened right there—that is what actually helps you move forward in fun and, honestly, in life.

Why did you quit having fun? There may be lots of reasons. And for many of us, it wasn't a full stop. Rather than prioritizing, thinking about, and choosing fun, we've just made it a leftover part of our lives that doesn't get considered. But for others of us, if someone asks what sounds fun to us, we don't have an answer at all. We can't remember when we last had fun, and we can't figure out how to do it again.

But you did as a kid. You did have fun. Think back . . . what did you do? Who were you with? What did you love? What made you laugh? What was fun for you?

CHASE THE FUN

Think back and ask yourself: When did I quit having fun? Spend a little time today journaling about the memory or stories that come to mind.

Rest Makes Way for Fun

> In returning and rest you shall be saved; in quietness and in trust shall be your strength.
>
> ISAIAH 30:15 ESV

The problem is that we are tired. All of us. We are tired because we live in a world with no *off* switch. You can check your social media any hour of the day, you can respond to emails or texts throughout the night, in many cities stores are open twenty-four hours and you can shop seven days a week. So while you may be sleeping at night (or maybe you aren't), as you're falling asleep and as soon as you wake up, you know.

You know you could be working. You know you could be watching. You know you could be searching or posting or answering or scrolling.

The more I talk with friends about fun, the more I realize we all need rest. We all need a separation from that 24/7 on-call culture. We all need a break. And while we want to prioritize fun, it feels extra challenging when we are tired.

So rest is a must. I'm not *just* talking about the sleep kind of rest, but I *am* talking about that. Your medical professional can tell you how many hours you need for your body, but getting enough sleep matters. Our bodies were meant to heal and rest and shift down for hours every day. And it is incredibly hard to choose fun when you wish you were sleeping.

Certainly there are seasons when your sleep is changed or interrupted or less than average. But one of the themes in our lives should be how and when we rest, how we prioritize that in our lives, so that fun has plenty of room to grow in our lives as well.

I know you are tired. I'm tired too. So this week, while we're looking for fun in our lives and in our calendars, let's make way for rest too. When we prioritize rest in our lives, fun has plenty of room to grow as well. Make it practical, put it on your calendar, and invite rest—whether that is a nap or a thirty-minute walk or a day away or an extra hour of sleep. Whatever rest looks like for you, find it. Chase it. Fun will be right behind.

CHASE THE FUN

Schedule some rest during the remainder of this week. Put it on your calendar!

How Do I Prioritize Fun?

> Don't be fooled by the calendar. There are only as many days in the year as you make use of.
>
> CHARLES RICHARDS

use both a paper planner and an online calendar. It takes a lot of resources to keep me organized. I write down EVERYTHING because my brain holds approximately none of the dates and times. Everything that matters most to me gets put on the calendar.

You may not be the type to write it all down or add it to the calendar on your phone or computer, but you put what matters most on the calendar of your life.

Midday, most every day, you eat lunch.

I have a friend who goes on a jog most days around 4:30 p.m.

Every meal and party and phone call goes on my calendar, in my own handwriting.

Every night, at some point, you lie down and sleep.

I know the things that are easy for me to fit in every day, like breakfast, lunch, dinner, and sleep. I also know the things that require me to be more intentional, like exercise and time with friends.

We show what we prioritize by what we make time for, by what we actually add to our calendar, our week, our plans. So maybe it is time to start putting fun in your calendar.

I know that may sound like a wild idea, but maybe this week, just put thirty minutes on your calendar for Saturday and label it FUN. And then start asking, "What sounds fun to me?" What would be fun in that thirty minutes? Who would you want to include? What activity might be the most fun in that window of time? What is something you've never tried before that sounds really fun? What's something you've long loved but haven't made time for recently?

The days leading up to that thirty-minute block on your calendar will give you time to brainstorm and chat with your people and collect any supplies you may need. (It's just thirty minutes anyways, right? You can watch a show in that amount of time!) By the time Saturday gets here, you have a plan. And by Sunday, you're thinking through what went great, what could go better, and how you'll refine your fun for next time. Put it on your calendar and see how that prioritizes and changes your fun!

CHASE THE FUN

When can you add thirty minutes of fun to your life this week? Put it on your calendar today!

What You Need to Have Fun

> Dream and give yourself permission to envision a You that
> you choose to be.
>
> JOY PAGE

’m a list maker and a calendar keeper. Organization is fun to me
(and necessary). And it’s time to make a real plan for you to chase
the fun in your own life. So today, as we dive deeper into the power
of fun and how to find it, we need to make a list of what you need in
order to have fun.

1. **Permission to not be great.**

   I’m giving you full permission to try something new, to
   be an amateur, to pick an activity that you do not know how
   to do and actually try it. You know that thing you’re really
   good at now that you’ve done it a ton of times? You were new
   at it once. There is so much pressure in our lives to be very
   good at everything. But trust me when I say that it’s okay to
   be new at something, to be not great at something, to be trying and failing. It will be more fun if you let yourself try new
   things and allow yourself to not be great.

2. Permission to fall in love.

Whether it's a new restaurant in your neighborhood or a recipe in an old family cookbook, fall in love with it. Maybe you've met a new friend or gotten a new pet or found a new route home. Fall in love with it. Do not feel the pressure from culture to play it cool, to tone down your feelings or hold back when something brings you joy. Open up your heart and let yourself love.

3. Permission to get a new hobby.

What is a hobby? We'll do a deep dive into that one later, but what matters most for now is that I am giving you full permission to make space in your life for a hobby. Maybe you haven't had one in years. Maybe you had a hobby but you turned it into a part-time job, a side hustle, or your career. Maybe you have never had a hobby and wonder what that would even look like in your life. Start talking about it with your friends and family—what their hobbies are, what hobby they think you would enjoy—and start feeling that permission you have given yourself to make a hobby a part of your life.

CHASE THE FUN

Which of these feels the most challenging for you?

What If I Can't Afford Fun?

Wealth is the ability to fully experience life.
HENRY DAVID THOREAU

When we think of fun, we imagine a season pass to an amusement park, a meal that costs as much as filling up an SUV's gas tank, or a flight across the country or around the world. We equate fun with big and expensive. And sometimes it is. There are times when I have to save up for weeks or months to do the thing I really want to do. There's nothing fun about debt; it traps you. The less I go into debt and the quicker I get out of it, the more space I have for fun. So, planning ahead, I also have to plan for fun in a way that doesn't trap me in a financial jail.

But I think one of the ways we miss fun is by assuming things about fun that aren't true—like that it always has to be big and always has to be expensive.

One of the best shows on television is a cooking show that has competitors pitted against each other using random ingredients. My sisters and I love watching that show, and a few years ago, we decided to play this competition in our parents' home on a holiday. We each had a different part of the meal that we were in charge of, and there were certain ingredients we had to use that were all found in the pantry. It was not expensive, we used ingredients we had, and we already were planning to make something for dinner—we just decided to make something FUN.

The invitation to have more fun in your life is a balanced invitation—some things you want to do will take more money and more time. But there are daily things, daily hobbies, that are cheap or free. Walking through a park, adding a special ingredient to a favorite recipe, helping a friend in their garden, driving to an unexplored thrift shop with a five-dollar bill in hand, using the local library, sharing board games and puzzles with your neighbors, scanning old pictures to create photo albums, picking back up a sport you let go of years ago. These are just a few ideas—you can come up with many more, I bet—of activities and opportunities that don't cost much while you save for the things that have a greater cost!

CHASE THE FUN

What's your favorite fun thing to do that doesn't require lots of money? Put it on your calendar to do sometime this week or next!

What If I Mess Up?

> Failure is simply the opportunity to begin again, this time more intelligently.
>
> HENRY FORD

There are some personality types who struggle with fun because they worry they will do it wrong. (Trust me, I have the emails and the DMs and the worried conversations with friends at live events to prove it.) Some of y'all are just pure concerned that you aren't going to be able to have fun, because in your mind there is a right way and a wrong way to do it.

What often happens when I ask people to tell me what sounds fun to them is they open with some sort of apology or explanation. Before they even tell me what sounds fun to them, they are concerned that I will judge their fun. That as the self-appointed and VERY highly trained Fun Coach, I am going to find their fun lacking.

But here's what is true: if it is fun to you, IT IS FUN. Full stop. Period. Truth. If it is fun to you, it is fun.

And here come the caveats. If it is fun to you, it is fun, unless

- your fun enslaves another person.
- your fun comes at the expense of another person.

- your fun does not align with your moral code or spiritual practices.

But ninety-nine times out of one hundred, that isn't why people fear their fun will be judged. They are worried—maybe YOU are worried—that their fun isn't fun enough or cool enough or that their fun is the wrong kind of fun.

I wonder who told you that we all need to approve of your life before you get to live it? I wish you could unhear that message, but that isn't how this works. Instead, I will offer you a truer message: You are allowed to be you. You are allowed to love what you love and pick the hobbies that interest you and chase the fun you want to have, all without getting anyone else's check of approval.

The most confident people are rarely the ones we expect—the most beautiful, the most wealthy, the most put together. Honestly, in my experience, the most confident people are the ones who are comfortable in their own skin and living fully into who God made them to be. You can do that too. Because your question isn't whether you will get fun right or wrong; I think your deeper question is whether you will be loved no matter what. And yes, yes you will.

CHASE THE FUN

Why do you sometimes feel like your
fun is judged by others?

How do I get over my fear of doing new things? | Lynn

What's the best way to step outside your normal fun and try something new? | Barbara

How do you begin again? Starting over is so hard. | Abby

What does it look like to pursue a relationship as an amateur? | Emilee

How can you be an amateur and not get "cancelled" for making mistakes? | Emily

How do you have fun in times of transition? | Kristen

How do you not feel embarrassed when you aren't good at your hobby? | Shannan

How do I stop striving to excel at a hobby? Thoughts around staying an amateur? | Jenn

When would I carve out time for fun? | Heather

BE AN AMATEUR

It Is Better to Be an Amateur

> You never know what you can do until you try, and very few try unless they have to.
>
> C. S. LEWIS

I am a professional at one thing: my job. That's it. That is the only thing in my life where it really matters that I be a professional. At everything else—every relationship, every activity, all of it—I'm an amateur. And it's actually better that way.

Often we use the word *amateur* to describe someone who makes a mistake or handles something incorrectly. Like when I get on the subway in New York City going the wrong direction, I just roll my eyes at myself and say, "Amateur hour FOR SURE," because what a dumb mistake to make. Or when I bake a cake and it totally flops because I'm trying to make something dairy-free and gluten-free, so it's not like a box of mix I can just dump into a bowl with an egg and some oil. But when the cake turns out more like a biscuit or a pudding—100 percent because of me, not because of the recipe—it's an amateur move. Because I don't know what I'm doing.

But the actual definition of *amateur* is so much better than that.

Amateur (noun):

- a person who engages in a study, sport, or other activity for pleasure rather than for financial benefit or professional reasons.
- an athlete who has never competed for payment or for a monetary prize.
- a person inexperienced or unskilled in a particular activity.
- a person who admires something; devotee; fan.*

Doing something for pleasure rather than professional reasons. Admiring something and being devoted. It's like we've taken that ONE meaning of the word—someone who is unskilled—and made it the ONLY meaning of the word. And by doing that, we've given it a negative connotation. When we hear someone say "amateur," we automatically assume they have screwed up. We forget that maybe they were just doing something for fun.

It is actually better to be an amateur—to let yourself do some things that are just for fun, just for pleasure. Let it be something you are devoted to, and don't require it to make any money. Something good will grow in you when you become an amateur again.

CHASE THE FUN

What is one area of life where you are an amateur?

*Dictionary.com, s.v. "amateur," accessed May 21, 2020, https://www.dictionary.com/browse/amateur.

Try Something New

> Man cannot discover new oceans unless he has the courage
> to lose sight of the shore.
>
> ANDRÉ GIDE

Somewhere out in the middle of nowhere Colorado is a souvenir shop full of T-shirts and shot glasses and stickers and magnets. And in the middle of the store is a spiraling staircase that leads many stories up to a balcony from which you can see multiple states.

I am afraid of heights. Like, all the way, all the time afraid of heights. So going up stairs to a not-so-reliable-looking balcony is not my first choice. But I am a huge fan of trying new things in case they may be fun. One of my life rules is that I don't let fear stop me from doing the fun thing. So as my friend and I stood at the bottom of the stairs, having already paid our two dollars to climb to the top, I gave myself a pep talk and started up.

My knees knocked the whole way. My breathing got short. I was scared. But I knew it had to be safe and it wasn't that high, so I just had to be louder as my own cheerleader than the volume of the fear voices in my head.

I got to the last stair, stepped out onto the platform, and the view was absolutely incredible. My friend and I stood at the top and laughed and took a million selfies and could see to a distance that was crystal clear and beautiful. It was so fun. But I had to do something I had never done before to have fun in a new way.

It takes a lot of courage to do something new. We have all gotten comfortable in the lives we lead, the hobbies we have, the places we go, and the things we do. But gracious, there is something so fun about trying something new—a new recipe, a new route home, a new hiking trail, a new puzzle, a new book, a new experience. Allow yourself the opportunity to feel that moment when you really have no idea what is going to happen next—because everything is new! It's a whole lot of fun to try something new.

CHASE THE FUN

What new thing are you going to try today?

Try Something Again

Ever tried. Ever failed. No matter. Try again. Fail again. Fail better.

SAMUEL BECKETT

When we recorded an episode of our EnneaSummer series on my *That Sounds Fun* podcast, Enneagram coach and expert Seth Abram mentioned how each Enneagram number has a different type of exercise and way of eating that works best for them. I had never thought about that, but I googled it as soon as our conversation was finished.

I discovered that Enneagram Sevens need to play. That clicked immediately. And my mind jumped back to a younger time in my life, a time when the soccer ball was never far from my feet, when rolling around on grass and slide tackling and chasing other players and the ball was the most fun I was having.

I hadn't played in a game since high school. Two full decades. But suddenly I knew what was missing from my exercise life: sports kind of fun. I wasn't having the kind of fun that felt connected down to my bones and down through my history. And I hadn't had that level of fun in exercise since the end of my senior year of high school.

So I started playing again. Covered in sweat and red-faced, with tears dripping from my eyes, I cried because that hour of soccer was SO FUN. I cried because my foot connecting with a soccer ball was also my guts connecting with something more—with middle-school Annie and with those outside games and the smell of the grass and the sound of a shoe sending a ball down the field. I was back there and I was happy.

It's all about connection anyways, isn't it? With God, with others, with ourselves—yesterday and today.

My first day back with a soccer ball wasn't easy. In fact, I felt a little bit like a fish out of water. It had been so long since I kicked a ball, besides playing in the backyard with the Barnes kids. I've watched hours of soccer on television or from a seat in a stadium, but the footwork is very different when it's your own two feet and they are the feet of an amateur. But even on that first day, even though I was clumsy and new again, I had a ton of fun.

CHASE THE FUN

What is one activity you could try again?
Write it down here, and then give it a go.

Try Asking for Help

> Ask for help. Not because you are weak. But because you
> want to remain strong.
>
> LES BROWN

One of my friends is trying to teach her two daughters resilience and perseverance. She wants to instill in them the I'm-no-quitter type of grit that will serve them well their whole lives. And so the mantra they've adopted to that end goes like this (pretend their last name is Smith . . . it's not, but just pretend): "Smiths don't quit. We try again, we try a different way, and we ask for help."

I love that she reminds them it's a good option to ask for help. Mostly because I know so many grown-ups who have a hard time with that.

Why are we so reluctant to ask for help?

As your self-proclaimed Fun Coach, I want to remind you of something that we all seem to forget pretty easily. *Everyone* needs a coach from time to time. *Everyone* needs a teacher. *Everyone* needs a guide. Especially when we're amateurs at something! When we want to learn or grow or get better at a skill or hobby, we need to ask someone for help who knows what they're doing.

When I played soccer in middle school, I had an awesome coach who I looked up to so much and who taught me all the intricacies of the game. I am no longer confused about what offside means.

When I'm making a recipe I've never tried before, you better believe that I follow the step-by-step instructions from my favorite cookbook.

When I want to learn new methods of blending eyeshadow and makeup contouring and highlighting, it's straight to YouTube I go!

Where did we get the idea so firmly implanted into our heads (and hearts) that we should just know how to do new things and automatically be good at them? Somewhere along the way, we've internalized that it's weak to ask for help. That it's too vulnerable to need someone to show us the way. That we have to just pull ourselves up by our bootstraps and be amazing with no training and practice.

It's a pressure that we can release. That unfair and unrealistic expectation has got to go. It's not just okay to ask for help; it's a great way to learn. The added bonus is that you give someone else a chance to share something they love and have practiced, to showcase their strengths and invest those into you. Asking for help is a pathway to making great connections with others and discovering fun along the way.

CHASE THE FUN

Try asking for help today. The more you practice, the more natural it becomes.

Be an Amateur at Friendship

The only way to have a friend is to be one.
RALPH WALDO EMERSON

It's really fun to make a new friend. To meet someone for the first time and feel those buddy sparks, the ones that tell you this person is someone you could REALLY hang with. YES TO NEW FRIENDSHIPS.

But also yes to old ones. Ben Rector has a great song about lifelong friends and how awesome it is to have people who have known you through a lot of seasons. I'm thankful to have a few friends from my childhood who are still big parts of my life today. What that allows me is a soft place to land, a place with people who have known me in a lot of different jobs and seasons and hopes and dreams and breakups and fresh starts and haircuts. They have seen a lot of haircuts.

We need both, don't we? Old friends help us stay grounded and remember who we are. New friends help us stay open and discover new aspects of ourselves and the world around us. But we can definitely feel like an amateur with both.

Have you ever let a few too many weeks or months pass between the last time you reached out to that old friend and when you think to reach out again? I know I have. It's easy to second-guess just how long is too long. To want to avoid the awkwardness of trying to explain, of feeling like you're starting from scratch.

And the what-ifs that come with new friendships can be paralyzing, right? *What if I'm myself and they end up deciding they don't want to hang out again? What if I say something that offends them? What if they get sick of me?*

It's funny to me that we never imagine happy endings to our second-guess moments. *What if we have a great time, create inside jokes, and make plans to hang out again?* OR *I know just how this will go—we'll pick back up right where we left off, as if no time has passed at all!*

Despite second-guesses and what-ifs, keep showing up. And keep showing up as yourself. Loving the things you love and being the uniquely crafted masterpiece God made you to be. When you do that, you're being a good friend to your new friends, to your old friends, AND to yourself. And THAT'S fun.

CHASE THE FUN

Take a moment to intentionally reach out to an old friend or make plans with a new friend.

Be an Amateur at Romance

Love is patient, love is kind. . . . It always protects, always
trusts, always hopes, always perseveres.

1 CORINTHIANS 13:4-7

D o you know something everyone knows nothing about? *Romance.* When a new relationship begins between two people, that thing—the spark, the connection, the interest—is brand-new. It has never existed before. And if it has never existed before, how can anyone be an expert at it?

Maybe one of you has had a lot of practice at dating or relationships. Maybe one of you is super confident with the ins and outs of apps and texting and first dates. But neither of you has had a lot of practice at THIS relationship. Neither of you can be completely confident about the ins and outs of THIS connection, because it's new, unique, and in process.

So, we all—hear me say ALL—have permission to be amateurs at romance. And that involves holding on to curiosity, letting go of unhealthy expectations, and being generous with grace.

When you hold on to curiosity, you ask a question instead of making an assumption. "Obviously this is going somewhere" becomes "Would you like to go out again?" If you're not sure, ask. There's no gain in pretending and playing games.

When you let go of unhealthy expectations, you open yourself up to surprise and delight, and you protect yourself from undue disappointment. You're not interested in setting up the other person or yourself for failure or hurt feelings. That's not kind to either of you. (Pro tip: This also works with roommates, friends, spouses, and employees.)

Being generous with grace means writing kind stories in your mind about what's going on. It's believing the best of yourself and of the other person. It's keeping short accounts by quickly apologizing and forgiving. And when a relationship just isn't supposed to continue, it means acknowledging that and moving on as a kindness to you both.

My married friends tell me that romance looks different from season to season as years pass and their journeys deepen. Whether it's at-home date nights after the kids go to bed or trying a new hobby together as empty nesters, the invitation to consistent curiosity, healthy expectations, and generous grace remains.

So, take a deep breath, let yourself be an amateur at romance, and have fun!

CHASE THE FUN

If you're in a romantic relationship, write a kind story about where that's at, or write a few sentences about what you hope for in a romantic relationship. What sounds fun to you?

Be an Amateur at Conversation

> Be gracious in your speech. The goal is to bring out the best in others in a conversation, not put them down, not cut them out.
>
> COLOSSIANS 4:6 MSG

kept thinking of the three sentences I wanted to say, and how to say them, and how I wanted them to be heard. I had made a list of the sentences and the words and all the things I wanted to say. I had never had a conversation like this before, and I wasn't sure how it would go.

New conversations are scary and require more courage than you think you have.

It could be a conversation asking your boss for a raise.

It could be a conversation with a partner wanting to end the relationship or take the relationship to a new level.

It could be a conversation around a table about racial injustice.

It could be a parenting moment, a teaching moment, a loving moment, or a medical moment.

Every one of those examples, and many more, invites us to be amateurs at conversation. That means releasing yourself from being perfect and professional and allowing yourself to be new and unseasoned in the conversation you need to have.

When you find yourself ready to lead a conversation as an amateur, a conversation you've never had before, I find that a script or a list can be really helpful. It guides you. It doesn't force you to say certain things, but it does relieve the stress and pressure of trying to remember everything you have never said before. Also, tell yourself now so that you can tell yourself then: it won't be perfect. You cannot predict how the person on the other side will respond to the things you say, so after your first few sentences, it becomes a Choose Your Own Adventure. Be brave enough for that. Be open to that. Be ready for that.

Sometimes we aren't the ones who plan the conversation. Sometimes we are invited or forced into it by circumstances or relationships. When you find yourself an amateur on the receiving end of a new conversation, remember to breathe. Remember to think before you speak. Remember to ask for clarity, ask for what you need, and ask for time. Be full of grace with yourself and with the other people in the conversation, and allow yourself to be new in these moments.

CHASE THE FUN

Practice the conversation you want to have. Let yourself start with, "Okay, so I'm new to this, but I really want . . ."

Be an Amateur at Saying Yes

If somebody offers you an amazing opportunity but you are
not sure you can do it, say yes—then learn how to do it later!

RICHARD BRANSON

The day I received an email asking if I'd like the opportunity to
interview Jennifer Garner for the podcast, my jaw dropped.
(Yes, this was THAT Jennifer Garner: the one who played
Sydney Bristow and thousands of incredible alter egos on the TV
show *Alias* AND who caused me and all of my friends to aspire to be
"thirty and flirty and thriving" through her performance in *13 Going
on 30*. That Jennifer Garner.) I was speechless. And that is not a pre-
dicament your girl AFD often finds herself in.

Not because I didn't want to talk to her. Not because I didn't want
to be friends with her. Not because I didn't think all my friends who
listen to the podcast would love hearing from her. But because I
had never interviewed anyone with her particular level and sphere
of fame. I was nervous. And that's not typical for me. I don't know
about you, but I have trouble finding the fun in situations when I'm
nervous. I felt like an amateur in that moment. And in the moments
leading up to my conversation with Jenn. (She told me to call her

Jenn. We're totally friends!) I even felt like an amateur in the middle of my interview with her. But I did it. I said yes.

It turns out that Jennifer Garner is just as lovely as she has seemed to be all these years that I've been a fan of hers. The interview went great! And ironically, she shared about a really sweet movie she was starring in called *Yes Day*, which is all about families finding opportunities to say yes to wild ideas and to see what happens.

The thing is, if we don't say yes to things that make us nervous, we steal the chance from ourselves to find the fun in them. We can give ourselves permission to say a nervous yes. To take a clumsy step. To be an amateur at agreeing to try things that make us a little uncomfortable, because we might just discover a gift on the other side. Perhaps saying yes will lead to a new friendship. Maybe it means you learn a new skill. It could also lead you to a firm stance that you will not, under any circumstances, say yes to that thing again. That's okay! At least then you know. All of your yeses don't have to become successes. Just let them have a chance to become fun.

CHASE THE FUN

Say YES to something today that makes you a little nervous. Keep an open mind and heart and just see what happens!

Be an Amateur at Saying No

Pay all your debts except the debt of love for others—never finish paying that! For if you love them, you will be obeying all of God's laws, fulfilling all his requirements.

ROMANS 13:8 TLB

Around our office, we like to occasionally and lovingly remind ourselves and each other of a simple truth: *No is a complete sentence.*

It's an idea I learned from author Anne Lamott (but I've seen it attributed to others too). Whoever originated the idea, I've certainly benefited from their hard-earned knowledge. See, it can be good for us to say yes to things that make us a little nervous. Those can be stretching and fun moments of discovery. It can be equally good to trust our own limitations enough to simply say no.

Not every invitation is meant to be accepted.

Not every opportunity is meant to be explored.

Even good opportunities and invitations deserve to be told no sometimes.

You don't owe anyone time, energy, or effort that you don't have to give. So even if you don't have a lot of practice at it, and even if it makes you worry that you'll disappoint someone you care about, you can say no. Saying no may not seem fun at the time, and you may feel like an amateur at it, but it CAN be soul-level good for you.

If you are tired, no is a complete sentence. It will allow you the rest you need.

If you are feeling burned out, no is a complete sentence. It will allow you a chance to refuel.

If you are feeling too busy, no is a complete sentence. It will open up space for what matters most.

If you just don't want to, no is a complete sentence. It will help you be a good friend to yourself.

It's not unloving to kindly decline, and you don't owe anyone an explanation. You don't have to defend your no. I'm not sure when so many of us began buying into the faulty narrative that we always owe others a lengthy, detailed explanation of why we are choosing to say no to an opportunity. It's just not the case. The Bible says we shouldn't owe each other anything but love. That's it.

And just like all of your yeses don't have to become successes, all of your no's don't have to be forever. (I know . . . it's a real shame that part doesn't rhyme. Oh well.) When you have reaped the rewards of saying no—the rest, the perspective, the margin you've gained—you'll have new space and time and energy to revisit those opportunities.

CHASE THE FUN

Say no if you need to. Notice the space it opens up.

Be an Amateur at Saying "I'm Sorry"

> Never ruin an apology with an excuse.
> BENJAMIN FRANKLIN

''ve never heard anyone say that their baby's first word was *sorry*.

Of all the phrases children pick up and repeat and mimic as they're learning to talk and exploring language, "I'm sorry" does not seem to be one that naturally flows out of our miniBFFs' mouths. Instead, it seems to be one we must teach repeatedly and have them practice regularly. Even then, it can be like pulling teeth to convince them to apologize.

In fact, there's a little script my mom used when she was teaching (ahem, forcing) me and my sisters to apologize to each other when we were little. "I'm sorry I [FILL IN THE BLANK]. It was [FILL IN THE BLANK]. Please forgive me. How can I make it up to you?"

So, conversations between me and my sisters frequently sounded like this: "I'm sorry I pulled your hair. It was hurtful and unkind. Please forgive me. How can I make it up to you?" Never mind that in my heart, my side of the dialogue often sounded a bit more defensive and blaming. Perhaps it contained a couple of accusations or excuses.

I had a lot to learn in that area. See, I was an amateur at apologies. We all were.

And even though my parents stayed faithful to teaching all of us kids about how to repair damaged relationships, to be honest, I still feel like an amateur at apologizing.

That doesn't mean I stop doing it. Sometimes I may avoid those tough conversations longer than I should. I may draft and rehearse and then edit and re-rehearse what I need to say. But ultimately, when I've hurt someone I love, I need to say, "I'm sorry." I need to own my role in it and do my part to repair what's been damaged.

Because the truth is, there isn't much that's more fun than having peace and freedom in your up-close relationships.

CHASE THE FUN

Say you're sorry when you need to today. Use my mom's script if you can't think of what to say.

Be an Amateur at Saying "I Forgive You"

Keep us forgiven with you and forgiving others.
MATTHEW 6:12 MSG

As difficult as it can be to say that we've been wrong and to apologize, I often find it even harder to say (and mean) "I forgive you." I'm just being honest here. The fact that it's tough for me to say those words is certainly not something I'm proud of, but it IS something I'm practicing.

See, that's what you do when you're an amateur at something. You acknowledge that it isn't a skill you're great at yet. You give yourself some grace and ask for some grace and extend some grace to others.

Ultimately, when I'm in a situation where it's time to forgive, I just think about Jesus. I think about how He lived this sacrificial, empathetic, curious, tender, compassionate life. In the Gospels (those first four books of the New Testament), one of the things the writers showcase over and over is how Jesus sees people. Notices things about them. Women, kids, people others tend to overlook or avoid. He slows down and makes time for them.

When you slow down and notice people, you can't help but also begin to understand their story. To see what might make them choose to do things differently than you would. To have some empathy for why they may have hurt you. And maybe open some doors for forgiveness.

Forgiveness isn't excusing the hurtful thing they've done. It's not even saying that you want to be reconciled and for your relationship to go back to how it was before. It's simply saying that you won't hold them hostage to the worst version of themselves. (I didn't come up with that on my own; it's another thing I've learned from Pastor Kevin.) I know I don't want to be held hostage to the worst version of myself. And I bet you don't either.

When I remember how many things Jesus has covered for me, forgiven me of—well, it helps me slow down to see people. To notice the hurt and the challenges others are dealing with that might have caused the bad day that might have caused the sarcastic remark that stung me or the choice they made that caused me to feel rejected. There's a certain freedom we find when we say "I forgive you." And finding freedom is a deep sort of fun.

We won't do it perfectly. We can't. We're amateurs at forgiveness. But that doesn't mean we can't practice it, right?

CHASE THE FUN

If there's someone you need to forgive, start practicing today. Whether it's in your heart or in a conversation with them, open that door. There's freedom on the other side.

Be an Amateur at Endings

> Every new beginning comes from some other beginning's end.
>
> SENECA (but also Semisonic)

I adamantly, defiantly, sometimes embarrassingly hate endings. I hate when the World Cup ends. I hate when a good book ends. I hate when a relationship ends. Sometimes I'll go ahead and start looking forward to the "next thing" just to avoid all the feelings I have around the ending of the "current thing."

I'm no professional at grieving, at letting go or facing endings, but honestly, none of us are. We are all amateurs at loving and losing, because each circumstance and situation is different. Every relationship that ends is different from the one before. Every friendship that falls apart pings unique spots of pain. When a person you have known and loved dies, the loss is unlike any other loss you've experienced.

In a way that people cannot see, there is a unique grief that comes from losing dreams that will never be fulfilled or jobs that you weren't hired to do or homes that are no longer yours. There are losses and endings no one else sees, grieving that is so deeply private that, while the rest of your life could look right in space and place, you know something profound is missing.

This is true for everyone. Every one of us. While we are all amateurs, we are not that different from our neighbor or friend or family member or archnemesis. We are all very new to grief and pain, every time, and we all know it.

But we also know the release of a laugh and the freedom of a smile in a heartbreaking moment. We know that there can be joy in grief. That's the magic trick here; that's the piece you have to search for and find and give to your people. Every time you provide a smile amid tears, every time you have cookies delivered to a teenager at the hospital just because you know she loves warm cookies, every time you think of that one little fun thing that may make someone else's day better, the people you are serving with your fun are getting a glimpse of the hope and the peace and the joy and the promise of Eden.

CHASE THE FUN

Look for the chance to (sensitively and caringly) bring a little bit of fun to someone who's dealing with an ending or grieving a loss.

Be an Amateur at Leadership

Do to others as you would like them to do to you.

LUKE 6:31 NLT

t isn't natural for anyone to be the line leader. It's why we switch kids around when they first get to school, and they each get a turn being the classmate who leads the line to lunch or to the playground or to the gym. Everyone gets a chance to lead.

The same remains true as we grow up. Everyone is leading someone. It's one of my favorite conversations to have with friends, particularly friends who feel like they aren't influential because of the number of followers they have on any given social media site. What we see in Jesus's life is that He had twelve guys He led closely and taught constantly, and those twelve began a chain reaction that changed the world. So when friends tell me that they aren't leading anyone or that they aren't a leader, I usually push back.

You might not lead a company. (You might.)

You might not lead a family. (You might.)

You might not lead in a classroom or a hospital or on a football field or stage. (But you might.)

But you are leading someone. And that can feel really scary when you don't have time to watch all the leadership master class videos or read all the leadership books or attend all the leadership conferences. But there is someone following you, listening to your stories, watching how you live, and they are learning from you. Whether it is your coworkers or your children or your followers on social media, they are shaping their lives through the influence you have in your own life.

You don't have to be perfect at it. You don't have to be a professional. You just have to pay attention to the people who walk with you and to the life you are leading. How fun is it to think about leading one person into a healthier, happier, more secure-in-themselves life? Release yourself from the pressure that you feel to lead perfectly. Instead, see your story as it already is—you are a leader, your life matters to someone else, and you are very capable of leading in a lot of ways!

CHASE THE FUN

Create confidence in someone you lead today by asking for their input on something in which they wouldn't expect being invited to share.

Be an Amateur at Learning

Learning never exhausts the mind.
LEONARDO DA VINCI

My favorite vacations are the ones where I rest and learn. Whether it is at a winery or a historic home, whether it is through a book or a guided tour, learning is incredibly fun.

There are many things in life that we take too seriously (I think), and being called a "learner" fits into that category for me. Professional learners are important to the growth and flourishing of culture and communities. We need people who give their lives to understanding more than we know today so their knowledge can help shape how we live. We learn from the past, we learn from new discoveries, we learn from the bottom of the ocean, we learn from outer space. And I thank God that there are people who spend their lives that way.

The majority of us, though, will not be professional learners, but we can be lifelong learners. We can develop a posture of curiosity about life and be confident there are ways to get answers to our questions.

Here are some things I am learning right now:

I am reading a book about a Palestinian family and learning about the lives of women in that culture.

I am learning to juggle (albeit slowly learning because it is significantly harder than I expected).

I am learning about King David through my daily Bible reading.

I am learning about racial reconciliation through some podcasts I listen to weekly.

I am learning to walk a new trail in my local park because I just discovered it.

I am learning to cross-stitch on black fabric instead of white.

I'm not full of knowledge about any of these subjects, and I'm not great at any of these skills yet. But I'm having a fun time learning. That's the permission we need to give ourselves. Permission to learn new things, new recipes, new facts, new skills. Allowing ourselves to be new and be uneducated and really enjoy the process of learning. Learning is worth making time for. Learning comes in a lot of shapes and sizes and categories. Keep choosing it, over and over, in your spiritual, mental, and physical life.

CHASE THE FUN

What is one thing you are learning right now?

Be an Amateur in Your Own Physical Health

A cheerful heart is good medicine,
but a crushed spirit dries up the bones.
PROVERBS 17:22

feel like I am my own favorite science experiment. After a few decades of trying to change my body and get it to look a certain way, I found freedom from that and have a new mindset. (Many thanks to Jess Connolly for her work about body shame and freedom.) I realized that I have had an unrealistic expectation of my body. It was to the point where even when I hit a goal I had set, as soon as I looked in the mirror, I would see a handful of ways to continue to change my body. That's a different thing to me than improving my physical health.

So, I'm on a journey to improve my health. Not to force myself to be a certain size or to spend lots of time trying to look younger than the truth my life calendar tells, but to have fun being an amateur in my own health journey.

Yes, I have lived in my body every day of my life, which should make me an expert. But I am not. Every day is a new day in my own skin, and every day is a new challenge to choose the right nutrients and exercise and get the right amount of rest in order to be healthy.

Some people are experts in muscle tone or caloric intake. Some people are experts in medicine or healing supplements. I respect all of their wisdom and need it in my life. But none of them have lived in my body, none of them know what it FEELS like in here. They can tell me to lean on certain food groups and stay away from others, but they don't know how it feels to wake up with more energy and alertness that are directly connected to what I ate the day before. Their wisdom and expertise are really important, and I trust the professionals I have invited to speak into my physical health.

But it's really fun to try new things—whether a new recipe or a new walk outside or a new class at the gym. Remember that the goal is not to reach a certain body size or shape but to have fun for your whole life. Stay as healthy as possible, try many new things as you learn and grow, and celebrate all the things your body CAN do today.

Chase the Fun

What's one new way you are thinking about your physical health today?

Be an Amateur in Your Own Emotional Health

Be kind to yourself.

ANDREW PETERSON

Almost a decade ago, I started counseling, going on a weekly or every other week basis. I didn't know how to talk about my feelings. I didn't know how to parse them out and organize them in any way that made communicating about them possible. And I didn't know what to do with them once I understood that they existed.

Of course, throughout my life, I knew how to say I felt sad and I felt worried and I felt happy. I just didn't really know how to dig any deeper than that. You gotta know this about me: historically, I do not like pain. I do not like digging too deep into my past, because what if there are things I have forgotten that are painful and are better left there? What if there is something that has hurt me but I don't know what it is? Why pick a scab when I don't have to? I recognize this is incredibly backward thinking, but it is how I learned to cope long ago—look away and it will go away. But counseling changed all of that. I learned that the best course of action is not to ignore; instead, it's wise to get the sickness out, sweep the corners, check the balance in your bank account, and start the hard conversation.

Through appointments with my counselor and a week at Onsite Workshops, a seven-day counseling intensive meant to help you do good, hard work on some of the deepest pains in life—the parts of your story you may not have picked but have shaped you and your decision-making—I have learned how to live with my pain. Not love it, not coddle it, but exist with it.

That doesn't make me a professional at therapy, though. Not at all. Every appointment is brand-new and unlike any other. I'm an amateur every time I sit down on that couch across from a wise, trained therapist. While I know how to walk myself in and sit down, I don't know where the conversation will go, and I don't know how she is going to respond to what I say, and I don't know how her response is going to draw out the next topic or thought from me.

In your own emotional health, be an amateur. Learn about yourself. Listen to yourself. Trust yourself. And share your story with others.

CHASE THE FUN

What is one story you would tell today
in a therapy appointment?

Be an Amateur at Faith

> Now faith is confidence in what we hope for and assurance
> about what we do not see.
>
> HEBREWS 11:1

It was the kids Jesus always wanted to be around. The ones who knew less, cared less, and performed less were the ones He always was saying He wanted closer to Him. I think we should pay more attention to this.

It was never the adults, the ones who knew a lot and had a lot of plans and ideas. They were not the ones Jesus told us to be like. He told us to be like the kids.

And kids are fun. A million things make them fun, but some of my favorite things about my miniBFFs are that they're curious, they're free, they're hopeful, and they're willing to be amazed.

When kids ask questions, there are legitimate question marks at the end of them. Children don't ask leading questions with ulterior motives and confirmation biases firmly set. They wonder with open minds and open hearts, and because of that, they can truly receive the answers to their questions. There's a gift in that. A chance to stay curious and keep wondering.

Kids are truly free. It doesn't occur to them to be self-conscious or to worry whether people are judging them. They're confident and they're not trying to prove anything to anyone. They feel secure to be themselves, to be (sometimes brutally) honest, and to accept others as they are.

Kids are hopeful, and they mean it. They approach life expecting to have fun, to be taken care of, to experience fullness.

Kids are willing to be amazed. In fact, they're hungry for it. There's this innocence and wonder to how they walk through their days, as if something wonderful is out there just waiting to be discovered. They're always on the lookout for it. And like my pastor Kevin Queen says, "We tend to find things we're looking for."

So, what if being an amateur at faith is simply approaching our journey with God like kids approached Jesus? We can be curious because He's big enough to handle our questions. We can be free because He's good enough to take care of us. We can be hopeful because He's faithful enough to hold our future and to keep His promises. And we can be willing to be amazed because He's amazing. If we're looking for Him, we'll find Him.

CHASE THE FUN

Ask God what you're wondering about today. Tell Him where you need some hope and freedom. Invite Him to amaze you, and then see what happens.

Be an Amateur at Creating

The desire to create is one of the deepest yearnings of the human soul.

DIETER F. UCHTDORF

We were always meant to make stuff, to take natural resources and turn them and flip them and combine them into something that matters to our planet and helps humans flourish. I mean, we are all made in the image of God, and the actual first thing we see Him doing in the Bible is creating. Day and night, earth and sky, sea and land, plants and animals, atoms and cells. The imagination, the order, the detail, the intentionality, the fact that He invites Adam into the process of naming the animals. All of it just fascinates me and makes me grin from ear to ear and maybe sometimes makes my eyes leak from sheer wonder.

Here's what I need you to hear, though: YOU. ARE. CREATIVE. You are. You have that in you.

And what you create, it doesn't have to fit into the traditional, conventional fine arts like painting or music or writing (though it can). Maybe you create paintings or stories or sermons or songs. Maybe you create warm and welcoming experiences for people with your gift of hospitality. Maybe you create spreadsheets that provide clarity. Maybe you create delicious apple fritters or other culinary masterpieces. (If you do, send me some. I'll happily taste test for you!) Or maybe you create playlists, choreography, chore charts, organizational tools, curriculums, or flower gardens.

The key isn't about specifically WHAT you create. It's more THAT you create. That you take the risk of investigating the spark that's in you, that thing you're passionate about or interested in or curious to know more about. And that you DO something with it. You don't allow it to simply stay an interest or an idea. Rather, you combine your interests and ideas with what's already in the world and you make something new. With your fingerprints all over it.

See, the world needs the unique thing that you make. It brings beauty, a smile, connection, new perspective. The difference it could make really matters. No one can do what you do. No one else can make happen what you make happen. So, even if you're new at it. Even if it feels clumsy. Even if it doesn't feel useful. Give yourself permission to create anyway.

CHASE THE FUN

What do you love to create? Spend some time doing that today.

Be an Amateur at Art

Every artist was first an amateur.
RALPH WALDO EMERSON

My grandparents went to an art museum and came home with pictures of the paintings, which my grandmother printed out for me and put into a photo album. I spent more time than you can imagine lying on the floor of my childhood bedroom flipping through the album of art. There was one particular painting, of men on a boat with a shark beneath them, that fascinated me. With my finger, I would trace over the brush strokes and the details, and it scared me and I loved it. Do you know what I mean? I couldn't look away.

Art does that, doesn't it? *Art* is a small word that covers a broad range of things: painting, music, drawing, sculpture, sign language, desserts, books . . . the list is endless.

What does it look like to start making art? Start with what you love. What art speaks to you? Is it the music you listen to or the food you eat? Is it the art in a gallery or a cross-stitch pillow? Start there. Even if you don't know how to do it, just start.

I think paintings are beautiful and moving and so powerful. So, for my sister's birthday a few years ago, we took a painting class together.

We painted multiple scenes of the mountains we could see outside where the class was held. My sister did an amazing job of mixing the mountain colors and matching the sky hues and creating an incredible piece of art. As for me? Disaster. I could not have created an uglier thing. I'm telling you, it made us all laugh how terrible it was. But I'm glad I tried. I'm glad I spent the time and the money to make the memory with my sister and give the art a try. I was an amateur—still am—and it certainly showed in my painting.

I've tried some other art that I'm also an amateur at, like cross-stitching. But I'm actually getting better at it the longer I do it. I've made a few pieces that I've gifted to family and friends, and I've made three pieces that are hanging in my house. Making beautiful art of any type—whether it is something we get to hear, see, taste, feel, or smell—reminds us of our creative God. It shows us again that all God makes is good and beautiful and true.

CHASE THE FUN

What kind of art do you want to make? Do a little research on how to do it, collect up what you need, and start creating!

Be an Amateur at Travel

The real voyage of discovery consists not in seeking new landscapes, but in having new eyes.

MARCEL PROUST

My group of friends travels together fairly regularly. With each trip, we predictably fall into our respective, unspoken roles. One friend is the activities coordinator, scoping out the sights to see, the restaurants to visit, the attractions we shouldn't miss. One is the double checker—kind of the mom of our little crew—making certain that no one has forgotten anything and that the door to the condo is locked when we leave. (She also always has snacks.) One is the time passer, curating road trip playlists and great conversation-starter questions, always with a "What if we . . .?" up her sleeve. And one, without whom no trip would ever actually move from dream to reality, is the planner, compiling the itinerary, ensuring the reservations are made, and making sure we know where to be and when.

Attempting to travel without the planner makes things . . . well, interesting to say the least. It calls to mind a solo trip I took to New York City a while back and a certain subway ride that was TENS of minutes longer than it needed to be due to the fact that *maybe* I wasn't on the correct train for my first attempt. Needless to say, there was an initial panic and some moments of stress, and then I got things figured out, corrected my course, and made it to my destination only a little shaken up. How people ever got anywhere before the cell phone era, I'll never know.

I didn't have some amazing serendipitous experience in the process. There was no epiphany that made it clear why being in a different place than I should have been that day mattered.

What did happen, though, is that I learned something about myself: I can get lost and figure it out and be okay.

Every time I go to a new place, I'm an amateur at that place. It's good for us to veer off our beaten paths. We gain confidence and resilience, and we have fun when we discover new places, people, foods, customs, smells, and cultures. New is fun. So, let yourself be an amateur at travel. You don't even have to go very far to find something altogether new or to connect with someone who can teach you all sorts of new things.

CHASE THE FUN

Travel down the hall and introduce yourself
to other students in your dorm.
Travel across the street and take muffins
to new neighbors.
Travel to a new restaurant and experience
the flavors of a different culture.
Travel to a new city or country and leave
space for a little wandering.

Be an Amateur in the Kitchen

> Do not be too timid and squeamish about your actions. All life is an experiment.
>
> RALPH WALDO EMERSON

It may come naturally for you to intrinsically know what seasonings to add to a soup and what vegetables go with those chicken thighs you have roasting in the oven. If that is you, I celebrate you. Keep going! Try new recipes, try new foods, try new cuisines from new areas of the world. Why? Why does it matter? It matters because learning and growing in the area of cooking has no bottom—there is no end to how you can grow in the kitchen. And cooking is truly one of the oldest ways that communities connect. Sharing food you've made brings relationship and healing. People are cared for and provided for and loved by how you feed them.

I've been working to get in the kitchen more—for myself and for the people I love. There's just something about putting your hands to ingredients and turning them into something new and hopefully delicious. At first I pulled out old cookbooks and googled recipes, and since it was all new to me, I followed them to the letter. And it was fun. It wasn't all successful or delicious, but I stayed on budget and saved time and really enjoyed it.

Then it went to a new level as I began to experiment with changing up the recipes to my own tastes. Would I like this soup better if the vegetables were roasted first? What if I swapped out sweet potato for white potato? (Amateur tip: don't.) I've now perfected a few soups and salads for myself that stay in a pretty constant rotation in my fridge and freezer. And in a way that I don't know how to explain to you, just like I didn't know how to explain it to my counselor, cooking started to heal me. Not heal or change my body, but after weeks of cooking in my kitchen, how I talked about and thought about and looked at my own body changed drastically. It's like everything just settled. The waves of self-hate that had been crashing on my shore at a high-tide pace went back out to sea as I stirred and chopped and roasted and waited. Love grew as I waited. What I thought I was gaining in better food and faster service by eating out and having food delivered, I was losing all along in healing.

Cooking did something to me, continues to do something to me, that I can sense really matters. Even if I don't know how to do it great every time, it's a practice that is good for my soul and my body.

CHASE THE FUN

Think of your favorite thing to cook, purchase the ingredients you'll need, and make it today for yourself or for someone you love.

Be an Amateur at Fun

> If a man does not keep pace with his companions, perhaps
> it is because he hears a different drummer. Let him step to
> the music which he hears, however measured or far away.
>
> HENRY DAVID THOREAU

I love asking my podcast guests what they like to do for fun. I love hearing the variety of answers, the many ways people have fun, and how often it involves other people, a twist in the story, or a memory worth making. I love it when people share what sounds fun to them when they introduce themselves in meet and greet lines or out at restaurants. I really love that there are three thousand examples of my friends' fun scattered throughout my book *That Sounds Fun*.

Something that happens sometimes, though, is this pause followed by a qualifier or a disclaimer. A person will say something like, "This may not sound fun to you, but . . ." Or they'll make an offhand comment like, "I know this isn't big and fancy and flashy, but . . ." As if we feel the need to apologize for what sounds fun to us. Or we're insecure about someone judging and comparing and disapproving of our unique brand of fun.

But here's the truth of the matter, and I mean this with my whole entire heart: if it sounds fun to you, it's fun. Period. Full stop. End of story. Whether it's simple and innocent. Whether it's involved and larger-than-life. If it sounds fun to you, it's fun.

Your fun belongs to you. You can't get this wrong. There's not a skills test to qualify and there isn't a certification process and there will not be a grade given at the end. So breathe that sigh of relief that comes with the freedom to be an amateur at fun. There's so much freedom here. Try something new. Try something again that you haven't tried in a while. Invite others into it. Try what sounds fun to them and see if it does to you too. Be a novice, and laugh at (and with) yourself as you learn and grow.

CHASE THE FUN

Look back over the last thirty days and reflect on what you've discovered about yourself. Where are you embracing being an amateur, and what fun have you had in the process?

How do you figure out what you are passionate about? | Beth

How do you judge when it's okay to fall in love with people? | Cayenne

I like to read, but is that a hobby? | Kelsey

What other rhythms has God called us to that I'm missing? | Sue

How do you experience fun with God? | Ciara

Wondering how to be an amateur in relationships without being embarrassed. | Andrea

How do you find your people? People to do life with and have fun with! | Jordan

How do I tap into the freedom of childhood? | Meredith

The Power of Falling in Love

Time is too slow for those who wait, too swift for those who fear, too long for those who grieve, too short for those who rejoice, but for those who love, time is eternity.

HENRY VAN DYKE

fall in love constantly. All the time. I fall in love with ideas and I fall in love with the laughter of children. I fall in love with movies and I fall in love with recipes. I fall in love with the waiter who describes a wine perfectly and I fall in love with the handsome single man who volunteers at church. I fall in love with meals and I fall in love with jackets from shops in Aberfeldy, Scotland.

And I'm not being insensitive or crass with the word *love* like they used to tell us in church—that people use *love* too liberally and don't really know what it means . . . blah blah blah. I absolutely mean this. I feel love big. I feel everything very big. I don't feel one thing small. I feel big happy and big sad. I feel big excitement and big yikes. I feel big anger and big love. It's just all big.

It's powerful to let yourself fall in love with something (or someone). It shows a level of vulnerability when you admit to yourself that the emotion you feel is love. For some reason, there's an understanding in Western culture, probably mostly in men but often in women as well, that says we have to hold back our love. Don't get too excited, don't get too into something, be balanced and cool and don't let anyone know how stoked you are. I'm calling a BIG NOPE on that, because that's not being wise; that's being scared. Scared to stand out. Scared to tell the truth. Scared to really like something that other people don't really like (that you know of).

It works to my benefit most days. My friends know I REALLY love them. The people I am with have no question about where I want to be. My favorite stores know it, and my favorite restaurants know it. My podcast listeners know it. They know what I love and who I love and what things cycle in and out of my life based on who I'm quoting and what I'm talking about. My heart is on my sleeve because, in the truest sense of the phrase, that is just how God made me. And it's powerful to live the way God made you.

CHASE THE FUN

What do you love today?

Love Requires Risk

'Tis better to have loved and lost than never to have loved at all.

ALFRED LORD TENNYSON

I love big, and it is always risky. I feel it in me even today. I've been intentional about walking toward emotional health these past few years. Counseling, whether it's weekly or monthly, has been such an important part of my healing and growth. My counselor and I have talked through some really challenging pains and decisions and I know, no doubt, that I am a better thinker, decision maker, faith person, friend, and romantic partner than I've ever been before. And here's what else is true—the big hasn't gotten smaller. I haven't felt things less. Ten years ago, when I started on this path of really wanting to get some help with my thinking and feeling, I would have thought that going to counseling would make my BIGs smaller. But it hasn't. If anything has changed, it is that the range of my emotions has increased. The depth is the same, but now I can call each emotion by its actual name. But they're all still big.

And I cannot hide it. Sometimes I wish I could. I wish I could tone down what I feel. It would certainly feel less risky. As I've matured, I have been better able to control my physical and immediate responses, but what I feel is still, well, big. A guy once told me that he knew exactly how I felt about him because I wear my heart on my sleeve. I don't know that he meant it as a criticism, but I'm fairly certain he didn't mean it as a blessing or a compliment. I was scared of that fact for a few weeks, and then I realized that, yes, whether I like it or not, my heart is absolutely positioned on my sleeve for all to see.

You want to learn to have fun? FALL IN LOVE. Fall in love over and over every day with something and maybe someone. Yes, it is going to hurt. But here's the thing about love and vulnerability and saying yes to the big feelings even when they are scary: it makes your heart beat hard and fast. And that's a good reminder that you are not dead. Because you aren't. The thing you thought would kill you did not kill you. You lived. You are living. And every time you fall in love with a new pair of shoes or a soccer team or a person who has treated you better than you thought you could be treated, may it remind you of how very alive you are.

CHASE THE FUN

Where does your love feel risky?
Journal about that today.

Why Do We Hold Back?

Life consists not in holding good cards but in playing those
you hold well.

JOSH BILLINGS

A h, isn't that the realest, truest question about love? Why do we hold our love back when we feel it, know it, and want to share it?

Sometimes we hold back because we lack the resources to love. Maybe we think the thing we want to love will cost us money and we lack finances. We hear it many times when couples are deciding when to have children—they want to wait until they have "enough" money, whatever amount they decide that is. They want to have children and to love them well, but they feel like they don't have what it takes financially. The same can be true with dreams or relationships or homes or opportunities.

We can also feel like we lack the knowledge to love. Maybe you want to try a hobby but fear you don't know enough to even start. Maybe a job description feels right in line with your desires but you don't even know where to start to walk toward that career.

There have been times when I have held back from loving because of the lack I felt relationally. Maybe it's your own emotional health that makes you feel like you can't love well. Or maybe it's your relationship history that makes you hesitant to try again.

What remains true is that when we want to love, there will always be something that whispers to us that we don't have what it takes to love well. And that should lead you to have a really healthy conversation with yourself. Why do you want to hold back? What do you feel like you are lacking? What would it look like to let yourself love, even if you feel fear?

To love well, to love fully, to really become the person you want to be and hope to be, you can no longer hold back your love. There is wisdom in how to love, for sure, and boundaries in love are healthy. But . . . more often we hold back because of what we fear and what we lack. I wonder how your life would be different if you didn't let your lack determine your love?

CHASE THE FUN

Where do you feel yourself holding
back when you want to love?

Fall in Love with Cooking

> Lots of people say food is medicine, but I would say cooking is medicine.
>
> CHEF CORY BARRETT

The time I interviewed Chef Cory Barrett on *That Sounds Fun* (episode 146) will long remain one of my favorite episodes we've ever recorded. Chef Cory was exactly the same guy in our conversation as he was on Food Network's *Spring Baking Championship*. And he was just as fun as I figured he would be. We learned all about the behind-the-scenes details of the competition and how he got into cooking and baking, and then he said a sentence I have repeated multiple times and that has stuck with me personally.

"Lots of people say food is medicine, but I would say cooking is medicine."

I needed to hear that. Even though he couldn't have known me well enough to know how much I needed to hear that, Chef Cory was preaching something important to me.

I have been living for years with the mantra "Food is medicine." Food will heal, food will heal, food will heal. Eat the right foods and your body will heal. But cooking as medicine? Maybe that's an Eden I didn't know I had lost. But when I heard it existed, I missed it.

So I started cooking a little bit more. I pulled out all of Danielle Walker's cookbooks, the family cookbook my mom put together a few years ago, and a few others I've had stacked around the house. And I began to make soup. Lots of different soups and stews. It's my favorite method of getting meat and vegetables into my body. I used the stove and the Crock-Pot and the Instant Pot. I made small one-person servings of soup and big pots that ended up in my freezer and fridge and in a few containers delivered to friends' houses as well.

Learning to cook is a rite of passage as we leave our childhood homes . . . otherwise you'll spend your whole budget on takeout (which you may do even if you know how to cook, BUT at least then it's a choice, not a necessity). But the act of cooking or baking, the time it takes to make something that didn't exist, and having it be something that is sustenance and fuel for your body—that is also good for your soul. Whether you are feeding a family of five, ten, two, or you, read through a cookbook, find a recipe that sounds fun to make, and give it a go (even if you're an amateur and it doesn't turn out just right).

CHASE THE FUN

Think of one food you love to eat and have never tried making yourself. Buy the ingredients and make it today.

Fall in Love with Learning

Let the wise listen and add to their learning,
and let the discerning get guidance.

PROVERBS 1:5

Being curious is one of my favorite things. The world is always brand-new when you get curious. When you start asking questions, when you start looking beyond what is right in front of you, that's when things get really fun.

I love Colonial Williamsburg. I love the tours they give—from the blacksmith to the Christmas wreaths, I am there for ALL OF IT. The way it makes learning history submersive, the way there are so many things I don't know about that time in our country's history, it's my very favorite. The last time I was there, the tour guide who took us through the capitol building kept mentioning side details—things like the number of swords on the wall or the year the flooring was installed. I'm not sure my brain retained it all, but it felt special to hear in the moment.

Have you ever done the Keys to the Kingdom Tour at Disney World? A few years ago, I got to tag along with my church's creative team as they did the tour and learned all about the creation, ideation, and growth of Disney theme parks. My favorite part was that, as we got on rides, we could hear our host through a little earpiece pointing things out to us, telling us stories along the way. The host made sure we saw lots of tiny details and found all the random Mickey Mouse ears that are carved into wood and outlined by flowers and sitting on the table, shaped by three plates placed like Mickey's face and ears, on the Haunted Mansion ride.

It remains true when it comes to spiritual growth as well. The more details I can learn, the more fun facts and connections that come to light for me as I'm reading the Bible or learning about Bible stories, the more fun I end up having. I honestly don't know how people did Bible study before the ability to search online! I bet I use an online resource most days in my reading time. I love to learn the root meaning of words that stand out to me in Scripture, I love seeing phrases as they repeat throughout chapters or books, I love seeing how certain authors use certain terms. As my curiosity grows, even if everything in Scripture doesn't make sense to me at first, my enjoyment of reading and studying grows. It's really fun to fall in love with learning—about people, about places, and new things about God.

CHASE THE FUN

Pick one person, place, historical event, or thing (any noun really ☺) that you love learning about and, just for fun, do a little research today!

Fall in Love with Growing Things

I don't know whether nice people tend to grow roses, or growing roses makes people nice.

ROLAND A. BROWNE

I've been in my head all morning about a situation that is moving slower than I wish it would. I want to know how the story ends, and I want to know what is going to happen next and when it is going to happen. But just to the left of me on my porch, there is a small plant that a friend gave me to celebrate the release of a book I wrote. And I'm realizing as I'm sitting here, there are two new stalks and a few new buds that didn't used to be there. The stalks are bright green, a way different shade from what was already there, and the buds are beautiful and tiny and an even more unique green.

Growing things is a fascinating task. I have done the watering, trying hard to follow the rules of not too much but not too little, and I set the plant in the sun, turning it every week or so to make sure all sides get the same amount of light. But I haven't done anything to make the new stalks grow.

The Bible talks about this—how it is our job to water but God's job to do the miracle work of growing. (It's in 1 Corinthians 3:6–7 if you want to read the passage.) And so we, in our everyday lives with our plants and gardens and relationships and careers and opportunities, should do our best to fall in love with the process of growth. The slowness and then the suddenness. The way tomatoes on the vine are green one day (perfect for fried green tomatoes) and red the next day (better grab 'em!) and almost too mealy the next. It happens in many areas of our lives, so appreciating the process in the things we can see will give us faith and hope in the growing situations that we cannot see.

That's what it takes, you know. Warmth, water, and faith. Something bigger and brighter shining on the thing, a little bit of whatever food it needs to grow, and faith living in you—faith that God will do the growing work, faith that things you cannot see are at work, and faith that the precious seed you hold in your hand will become exactly what it is meant to become.

CHASE THE FUN

What is one thing in your life that you see growing? To remind yourself that things are growing that you CAN'T see, go spend some time looking at plants or animals or cute kids to see growth in your everyday life!

Fall in Love with Being Outside

Everybody needs beauty as well as bread, places to play in and pray in, where nature may heal and give strength to body and soul.

JOHN MUIR

A few years ago, I started hiking pretty regularly at a place in Nashville called Radnor Lake. It's a beautiful natural park in the middle of the city, with a lake (duh) and hills and paths and all sorts of wildlife. It has been a great use of about an hour of my day, a few days a week, to go walk at Radnor Lake, up the trails that lead to the top of the hills and back down. Around the lake, getting to pass my favorite bench (#10), and then back to my car. I just love being there.

And one thing that can be frustrating but is actually really good for me, too, is that you aren't allowed to run at Radnor Lake. The short little part from the parking lot to the trail entrances—the part that used to be a road people could drive from Granny White Pike to Franklin Road—you can run on that part. But that's it. The rest you have to walk.

I don't like walking—it feels like it takes too long. I'm not great at running, and honestly, I don't run much faster than I walk, but it feels like I'm getting more accomplished. But when I am outside, whether it is at Radnor Lake or just walking around my neighborhood, I pay a lot more attention to the world when I move a little slower. I see the geese and their goslings. I see the flowers that have changed since the last time I was passing by, and I see the new for sale sign on my neighbor's house. Whether it is sunny or cloudy or cold or rainy, warm and bright or windy, I love spending a few minutes breathing fresh air and seeing the world move.

Just yesterday, after a few hours of working inside, I said to my coworker, "I just need to breathe outside for a few minutes." It wasn't that anything was going wrong or things were bad; I had just spent lots of time under office lights and breathing office air.

There's just something about getting outside. A short walk. A few minutes in the garden. Reading a book on the porch. A few hours by (or in) the pool. Walking a few blocks to the bagel shop. Parking a few spots farther back at the mall. The more you are in nature and the more you see, hear, and smell the real world, the more you will crave it, the more you will see God in it, and the more you will love it.

CHASE THE FUN

Take five minutes to walk outside
today, and notice five things.

Fall in Love with Books

When I get a little money I buy books, and if any is left I buy food and clothes.

ERASMUS

N ow, listen. I'm not saying you have to love reading (though I consider reading one of my all-time favorite hobbies). But I think you should definitely fall in love with books. You can read a book made of paper, you can read it on your e-reader, you can listen to an audiobook. All are totally fine.

I laughed yesterday as I scrolled through some memes and saw one that was a picture of a typical elementary school reading log. And across the top of the picture, someone had typed "This is when we first learned to lie." That got a real laugh out of me, because as a student, I remember lying to my teacher, and as a former fifth grade teacher, I definitely remember the children lying to me. It's not that we aren't buying books; lots of people still are. It's more that the time we once used for reading—right before bed, on a Sunday afternoon, on a flight across the country—we now use to scroll on our phones or watch Netflix or scroll some more. And the science around what those bite-sized pieces of text have done to our brains and our attention spans . . . well, it's not great.

So, let's fall in love with books again, not only because of the history of the printed word and the way books have stacked on shelves for generations but also because we need to stretch our attention spans again. We need to be able to start a story and not have it finish in minutes. We need to love the journey of reading a book, the pages turning (or the swipe of a finger on an e-reader or the switch to a new chapter on an audiobook), the anticipation of what could happen in the next chapter or on the next page, the appreciation of the work the author has done to form not just a well-crafted paragraph but an entire book.

There are no rules here. Read as many or as few books as you want. But don't give up on reading books. We need them. We learn from them in many ways.

CHASE THE FUN

What is your all-time favorite book? Why? Pull it off the shelf today and read a bit—or the whole thing!

Fall in Love with the Bible

The Word became flesh and made his dwelling among us. We have seen his glory, the glory of the one and only Son, who came from the Father, full of grace and truth.

JOHN 1:14

Of all the books I hope you will love, I hope you will love the Bible. It's an ancient text, published and reprinted and purchased more than any other book in the history of the world. Sixty-six books. Thirty-nine in the Old Testament, the story of the beginning of the world up to a few hundred years before the birth of Christ. Twenty-seven in the New Testament, which tells of Jesus's birth, life, death, and resurrection, the start of the church, the growth of the church, and even some words on where the world goes in the future and the return of Christ.

The Bible is a complicated book. I won't pretend otherwise. There are parts of the story that don't always sit well with me, and it contains heartbreaking stories and difficult passages that don't always make sense in our modern Western culture. But the whole thing is true. Every word can be trusted. In any book it's important to wrestle with the words you read, but particularly in books that will shape your life. But it's very safe to wrestle with a text that is thousands of years old and all the way true. It will not bend, it will not break, and what happens in the wrestling will actually make you stronger.

I don't know how I would do my life without the Bible. It gives me so much hope, so much understanding, so much peace. I read the stories of people like me, people who were trying their best but messed up pretty frequently, people who didn't know the end of their story either. I read stories of people attempting to honor God with their lives through the good and the bad days. And through the Bible, we get to know Jesus. And when we know Jesus, we get to know God.

The Bible is living and active—it isn't like other books you read. It does not change, but through the Holy Spirit, the Bible can speak to your life right here, right now. Test it and see for yourself. Spend ten minutes a day reading the Bible—maybe right after you read this book each day? And by the time we get to day 100, see if the Bible means more to you than it did when you began. Because God wants to speak to us and often uses His Word to do so, the Bible will absolutely speak to you today, right where you are.

CHASE THE FUN

Do you have a favorite verse or story
in the Bible? What is it?

Fall in Love with God

Where Christ is, cheerfulness will keep breaking in.
DOROTHY L. SAYERS

The world is full of challenges and hard days. I have found that there are mornings, afternoons, and evenings when I wonder why things can be so hard at times. Whether it leads to tears or just a deep sigh, I feel it.

And then the next moment, the next thing I say to myself, the next reminder is that God is kind. God is good. A counselor here in Nashville shares a mantra with his clients: "Life is tragic. God is faithful." That helps me a lot, to say that over and over to myself. It reminds me that the experiences I am having are human and that the God I follow is good.

There are so many good things about God. He is genuinely so easy to love. You can see God's fingerprints in every tree and flower and bird and human. You can hear Him in music and wind and thunderstorms and long conversations. You can feel Him in the ocean and in a hug and under a heavy blanket.

He's kind and loving and close. He's attentive and caring and real. He is mysterious and just. He is better than you can even imagine.

This—this falling in love with God idea—is not a race, and it isn't always immediate. You don't have to go from meeting Him to loving Him. But as you get to know Him, as you read the Bible and learn more about God's personality (starting in the Psalms and in the book of John will be helpful), my guess is you will grow to love Him. When you learn what He is really like, how intimately He cares and is involved in our lives, when you see His hand and hear His voice and realize how incredibly great the Creator is, you can't help but love Him.

CHASE THE FUN

What are some words you would use to describe God? List five of them in your journal.

Fall in Love with Wisdom

If any of you lacks wisdom, you should ask God, who gives generously to all without finding fault, and it will be given to you.

JAMES 1:5

Trying to do life alone is incredibly hard. When it comes to making decisions, figuring out the right next step, and sorting out the correct move to make, doing it alone is almost impossible. So we invite others in. Even at the risk of looking dumb, even if it makes us vulnerable, we need the wisdom of others to help us make the right choices.

Don't let decisions strangle you. If you are choosing between burritos and tacos, you can do it. I believe in you. You don't need a committee to vote. But in decisions that are weighty, that have cost attached, getting outside wisdom will help you see and know what you don't naturally see or know.

The Bible talks a lot about the power of wisdom, our need for it, and how God will generously gift it if we just ask. It's a prayer I say almost daily—asking God to increase His wisdom in me, to help me know what I don't know, to lead the right voices into my life to help me when I'm trying to do my day well and wisely.

Falling in love with wisdom will save you a lot of pain. It will save you a lot of heartache. It will also save you a lot of time and probably money and definitely apologies. Wisdom won't protect you from all hurt, and it certainly won't make your decisions or behavior perfect, but it will make things better.

So where do we find this wisdom to fall in love with? Start with God, start in prayer, and start in Scripture. The book of Proverbs is perfect for this—thirty-one chapters, one for each day of the longest months of the year. Adding a chapter of Proverbs a day to your routines and disciplines will increase the wisdom that lives in you.

We can get wisdom from the people around us too. From the ones who speak into our lives, from Instagram accounts we trust, from a pastor in the pulpit or a writer in a book. Some people know more than we know. Find those people and let their voices help you move and grow and fall in love with wisdom.

CHASE THE FUN

Who are some of the wise people in your life?
Seek them out today, ask for what you need, and
thank them for their wisdom in your life!

Fall in Love with Quiet

Take time to be quiet.
ZIG ZIGLAR

If you and I are friends, this essay, this topic, is already laughable to you. "Annie is telling ME to fall in love with quiet? Annie, the loudest friend I have? LOL." I know, I know. But for many of us, the volume of our lives has less to do with the amount of words we say or how loud our voices can get. The volume of our lives is determined by how much of life we fill with sounds.

None of the sounds are bad, probably. Music is wonderful. I love to listen and sing along and mean every word—and you can bet if I'm this loud of a talker, I'm a BELTER when it comes to singing. Even now, as I'm writing, college baseball is on the television as my background noise. So that's what I'm currently hearing.

But I've also opened social media a few times today, and those voices are loud. The podcasts I play when I'm washing my face and the Netflix I put on while I'm making lunch—it's all loud. The articles I read, the apps I refresh, the calendar I keep, the news that doesn't stop and the world that doesn't slow down and it is up to me to decide how loud my life is.

In 2020, when a global pandemic stopped the world, my life got suddenly and literally quiet. I wasn't married and had no roommate at the time, and without the ability to visit and meet up for dinner with friends, my life got lonely. And quiet. And those first few days were sad and scary and unlike anything I had ever experienced. But then I turned off the television and I pulled a puzzle out of the cabinet in my living room. And things slowly started to change in my life.

We spent months like this, alone in our lives. And when the restrictions eased and we began going back out into the world, I got asked the same question in a lot of interviews: "What did you learn in the pandemic?" And the truth is that I learned to love the quiet. I can't believe that is my big takeaway, but it is. The quiet in my calendar led to a quiet in my life. The quiet on my phone (my choice) led to a quiet in my mind and home. The more I chose the quiet, the more I loved it. The more I grew. The more I rested.

CHASE THE FUN

How can you make your life a little quieter today? Take one action step today to quiet some part of your life.

Fall in Love with Slowness

The trees that are slow to grow bear the best fruit.
MOLIÈRE

There are a few things I'm known for: Fun. My loud laugh. My love of soccer. My utter lack of chill when it comes to Dolly Parton. But I am NOT known for my patience. I don't usually move slow, so it kinda makes me crazy when things around me move slow. I think fast. I talk fast. I feel fast. I make decisions quickly.

Slowing down does not come naturally to me. Waiting takes effort, and I usually get too much in my own head, crafting elaborate stories of what might happen and how things will end up (often involving worst-case scenarios or beautiful happily-ever-after endings), which causes me to become even more impatient.

It's not that there aren't great aspects of moving quickly; it's just that you can't fall in love with slowing down if you don't give it a try. And, believe me, there are benefits to slowness. Here are some things I've been learning about what happens when you slow down.

You don't mess up your freshly painted nails.

You have time to think.

The cake is perfectly baked—it doesn't cave in on itself nor is it dry and falling apart.

You notice new blooms on plants in your neighbor's yard.

You don't buy things you later regret buying.

You have space to listen when you ask someone, "How are you?"

You overhear people saying funny things in line at the store.

You get richer, more complex flavors the longer the sauce simmers.

You can interact with the clerk ringing up your groceries.

You are grateful for what you have because you take time to notice and appreciate it.

You understand the actual value of what you're waiting for.

Learning to slow down and wait well involves equal parts gratitude for what you do have, hope for what will come, and perspective that, no matter how slow things feel, you can trust God is always right on time.

CHASE THE FUN

Today, do one thing a little more slowly than you typically would, and take notice of what feels different.

Fall in Love with Your Spiritual Journey

The journey of a thousand miles begins with a single step.
LAO TZU

I grew up thinking there was one outline, one journey, one prescriptive way for having a daily relationship with God. It's not that anyone taught me that overtly; it's just that what I saw and experienced seemed to indicate there was this linear progression that began around age five and then your spiritual journey was pretty well mapped out from then on. It went something like this: make a public profession of faith as a child, get baptized around age eight, go to youth camp and rededicate your life to Christ every summer, stray a little and sow your wild oats sometime in high school or college, get married the second you graduate from college, come back to God, and stay involved in church from then on.

Imagine my surprise to find out there's no prescribed path. You can meet Jesus and know Him just as truly at age five as you can in your fifties. Everyone does not actually go off the deep end and party hard in college. (For me, they were some of the most personally transformative years of knowing the Lord more deeply.) Not getting married at twenty-three does not mean God's plan for your life is over.

Your journey with Him is just as unique as you are.

Now, don't get me wrong. I DO think there are rhythms and practices that can benefit everyone's relationship with God—things like talking and listening to Him in prayer, reading the Bible, practicing Sabbath regularly, being an active part of a body of believers—but these aren't checklist obligations. These are chances to know and be known by Him, invitations to spend time with and rest in Him, and ways to trust Him with your life.

I also believe you get to adventure with God about what time of day you love spending time together. And whether it's walking in nature or listening to worship songs or reading a book with other people or journaling or some combination, all of these support your efforts to get to know Him better.

In a similar way to how you enjoy doing different activities with different friends—and that can even change with the same friend through different seasons—your spiritual journey with the Lord gets to be just that: yours and His. Here in the South, we would say it's "y'all's." So fall in love with that journey. Even when it's one step forward and fourteen steps back. It's still you and Him. He never fails and He never leaves.

CHASE THE FUN

Do one thing with God today that
you have fun doing with Him.

Fall in Love with Your Body

> The LORD does not look at the things people look at. People look at the outward appearance, but the LORD looks at the heart.
>
> 1 SAMUEL 16:7

Every now and then when I'm hiking at Radnor Lake, instead of focusing on the beauty of nature around me, I'll focus on my body. Starting at my feet, I'll take this inventory and just kinda notice all the things my body is doing in that moment that are good. My toes are helping me balance. My feet take steps and move me forward. My legs are strong and hold me up. My lungs and heart are working together to breathe and beat and deliver all the oxygen and blood I need to keep moving. My nose takes in the scents of the woods, my eyes focus on the details of creation, my ears tell me what to pay attention to.

This little practice helps me stay grateful. See, just like you, I'm inundated with messages about my body every day from every direction, and they can plant little seeds of dissatisfaction, disappointment, and disillusionment with my body's shape, size, age, height, weight, and abilities.

The body you have—it's a gift. An exclusive one that you only get once. It's the one you've got, and it's gotten you this far. You and your body have made it to today together. No matter your body's size, shape, or abilities, there's something I know is true about you: you are made in God's image. AND He calls you a masterpiece! (Read Ephesians 2:10. And don't even get me started on all the ways that word *masterpiece* can be translated: handiwork, workmanship, work of art, creative work, creation, poetry!) You're a picture of God moving about in the world. How cool is that? You know who else was one of those? Jesus. The Bible says in the Gospel of John that "the Word became flesh and dwelt among us" (1:14 ESV). He knowingly made that choice because of how much He loved you and me . . . bodies and all.

So, what does it look like practically to fall in love with your body? I think it starts by being a good friend to it. Feed it good things, move it to keep it healthy, say kind and grateful things to it, give it lots of rest and hydration, be patient with it as it changes.

Like our friend Jess Connolly says, "You have a good body." Remind yourself of that daily. (Jess was on episode 303 of the *That Sounds Fun* podcast if you want to hear more of her brilliance!)

CHASE THE FUN

Take a little inventory of your body and be grateful for all the ways it is good.

Fall in Love with Exercise

Just keep swimming.

DORY, *Finding Nemo*

H ere's what this day is NOT going to be: guilting, shaming, or "shoulding" you about working out. I'm not going to prescribe you a number of times a week. I will not advise you on the types of exercises you should do. I will NEVER tell you that you need to lose weight. I am not that friend.

I will tell you this: taking good care of your body and doing things to stay healthy and strong is fun! When you move your body, you get better quality sleep. When you're well rested, you have more energy and increased focus. That means you get things done. And then you have more time (that ever-elusive resource we can never quite find enough of) for fun!

But exercise itself can be fun too. I go through seasons when my favorite way to move my body is hiking at Radnor Lake. During COVID, I did a whole couch-to-5K program that got me motivated and moving in a different way from what I usually enjoy. I had fun researching the gear, following the plan, and trying new things to see how they impacted my running experience. Playing soccer is one of my favorite ways to exercise, partly for the competition, partly because it's communal, partly because it connects me to my younger self and some really great memories.

But your fun exercise doesn't have to look like my fun exercise. What kind of exercise sounds fun to you? Sometimes the only way to know the answer is to try some different things. Is group movement your thing? Try a Zumba or hip-hop dance class. (If you have the coordination. Sadly, I do not.) Are you competitive and love to be pushed? A spin class or a personal trainer might be a good choice. Do you have that sports gene in you? Rec league tennis, basketball, or soccer just might be your jam. Do you love to check things off a bucket list? Create a bucket list of hiking trails or parks in your area to tackle!

Falling in love with exercise IS possible. Just let yourself try different things until you find what sounds fun to you. When it sounds fun, then you're more likely to stick with it. And then it stops being a chore or a box to check and starts to simply be a fun part of your life.

CHASE THE FUN

Experiment with a new or different activity
or exercise and see if it's fun for you.

Fall in Love with Fruits and Vegetables

> The best place to find God is in a garden. You can dig for him there.
>
> GEORGE BERNARD SHAW

Have you ever cut, chopped, or diced a red onion? If the onion wasn't already causing my eyes to puddle, I could tear up at the beauty of it. The concentric circles of alternating deep purple and stark white. How the tiny pieces hold on to each other until you separate them.

Or have you participated in a contest to see who can spit a watermelon seed the farthest? Have you walked through the stalls at your local farmers market and noticed the rainbow of veggie delight when the mountains of heirloom tomatoes, eggplants, summer squash, and zucchini are piled high, and how the farms and farmers all have these rich histories that feed the soul as much as their produce feeds the body?

And as a native Georgian ("Go Dawgs! Sic 'em!"), I'd be remiss if I didn't mention the particular flavor of heaven that you experience when you bite into a ripe Georgia peach from the Peach Truck and let the juice take a stroll down your chin before you catch it with your napkin (or the back of your hand . . . you do you).

Here's the thing we learned when our friend Simoni Kigweba was on the podcast way back in January 2018: there is a special nourishment we get from the fruits and vegetables the earth produces. And there's a certain magic to it when they're local and in season. I've never done it before, so I could be wrong here, but I imagine there's a real sense of satisfaction that nourishes places deep in your heart when you eat produce you actually grew with your own two hands!

In Eden, gardening was one of the first things God invited people into. Cultivating the soil, the cycle of the seasons, the benefits of the patience it takes to grow things, and the reciprocal life-giving properties veggies and fruits offer to us as humans. It's just beautiful. And I don't want you to miss it.

Fall in love with fruits and vegetables. Try them in season, prepared different ways. If you're partial to red delicious apples, give pink ladies a shot. If you usually do vine-ripened tomatoes, try roma for your next recipe. Don't sleep on bing cherries for the five minutes they're in season. Do a little research on local farms, farmers markets, community gardens, or community-supported agriculture in your area. When you do, I promise you'll find at least one fruit, veggie, or farmer to fall in love with!

CHASE THE FUN

Do an apple tasting with friends. (It is legit SO FUN.) Buy several varieties, slice them, try them, and have everyone report on their favorites.

Fall in Love with Your Home

Home is the nicest word there is.
LAURA INGALLS WILDER

think when we go looking for fun what we are actually looking for is home. We are looking for peace. We are looking for simplicity, something to fill that spot that has been left by growing up or growing out or moving on. We may think we want fun, but what we really want is Eden.

While we can't have Eden this side of heaven, we can create spaces within our homes that point to the things we long for about paradise. At the risk of sounding like a good ol' alliterative preacher, I have three P's for falling in love with your home:

1. Peace
2. Personality
3. People

Peace: When it comes to the look and feel of your home, think about what brings you peace. Is it a certain color? Match the paint for your walls with that peaceful hue. Is it plants? Assemble the clay pots and get to growing! Is it cushy textures or gorgeous art? Load up on throw pillows and poufs and blankets or moody prints or bright canvases.

Personality: When it comes to style, you will feel most at home in your home when it feels like YOU. Utilize the pieces that showcase your uniqueness, whether someone else would say they're on trend or not. Include pictures and mementos that remind you of your roots or of significant, defining moments in your life. Arrange your books by color like our friend Emily P. Freeman does, if that floats your boat! Just let your home be an extension of the fun and unique aspects of YOU.

Side note about home design: There are definitely obstacles that can stand in the way of designing a haven. Get all you need from Pinterest and fun design accounts online, but stay true to yourself AND be patient. You don't have to do it all at once. You cannot live peacefully if you have outkicked your coverage financially. THAT is most assuredly not fun.

People: The people you share your home with make up a huge part of the equation when it comes to falling in love with your home. They may include your family, roommates, friends you invite over for dinner or to watch your favorite team play, or your neighbors. The key is to stay intentional about what you want the tone and atmosphere of your home to be.

CHASE THE FUN

Invite a friend who "gets" your style to shop with you for one signature piece to spruce up one of your spaces.

Fall in Love with Change

If you change the way you look at things, the things you look at change.

WAYNE DYER

t's a little funny to me how often I hear myself say that I want to stay curious and teachable but then my gut reaction when I hear the word *change* is to bristle and resist. Because aren't those all really forms of the same thing? Differing degrees on the same spectrum? I think they are.

So, why are we reluctant to give in to change in our lives?

I heard a wise pastor talk about this once. He said there are two types of change that we face in our lives: change we WANT to make and change we HAVE to make. We welcome change when it's something we want, right? When it's a promotion at work. When it's the home we've always dreamed of. But it gets trickier when there's change we know we need but don't necessarily want. Change we HAVE to make. Like when your doctor says you're going to feel better if you cut out this certain food. Or when a move to a new city is right for your family but means leaving dear friends behind. And it's especially tough to face change when it's not your choice and when it's out of your control. When you lose a job or experience the death of a loved one. Hear me, friend: I get it. NO ONE enjoys feeling out of control.

The way to fall in love with change is to trust the process. That's a phrase they teach at Onsite, a therapy center just outside Nashville where they host all sorts of workshops and programs that help people live healthier, more centered lives. Trust the process. See, change is simply that: a process. It takes time and can hold discomfort. It requires more from us than we realize we have in us. But it always, ALWAYS contains a gift. There's a gift for you in it, if you'll be patient and keep digging and trust the process.

The best news of all, when you're facing change, is that you're not alone. The God who created you and loves you also loves to finish what He starts. That's what Paul writes about in Philippians 1:6, where he says, "He who began a good work in you will carry it on to completion until the day of Christ Jesus." He starts good things and sticks with us all the way until they're done. Finished. Completed. Perfected. So, with that as our anchor, we can fall in love with change.

CHASE THE FUN

Think about a change you've walked through and how you grew through it. In your journal, reflect on that change and a current one you are experiencing, and see how you can encourage yourself with your own history.

Fall in Love with Failure

I never once failed at making a light bulb. I just found out 99 ways not to make one.

THOMAS A. EDISON

was listening to a podcast one day, and it was a conversation among four actors just shooting the breeze about their careers. As their conversation meandered, one of them said something that really stood out to me: you can't be great at something unless you're willing to be bad at it first.

I think this idea struck a chord with me because of how much I've thought about the importance of giving ourselves permission to be amateurs. Remember the definition of *amateur*? Doing something for pleasure rather than for professional reasons. Admiring something and being devoted to it.

But falling in love with failure takes that idea a couple steps further. If there's joy in letting ourselves be amateurs, then there's freedom in letting ourselves fail. Every risk has a fifty-fifty chance of resulting in failure. And I'd wager that the only true, lasting failure is when we stop trying.

Failure may not be the ONLY way to learn, but it is definitely a GREAT way to learn. It's what rewires our brains to do something a different way, to take a new approach next time. It helps us stay humble, reminding us that we don't know everything (nor should we). That humility helps us stay curious and ask things like "What would make this better?" and "Who could I invite into this with me?"

Don't take yourself too seriously. Whether it's a flop on a new recipe you tried or a relationship blunder that you need to make amends for or anything in between. Falling in love with failure is about acknowledging that failure always has something to show us and always serves to grow us.

CHASE THE FUN

Write down what you learned from the last time you dealt with failure. Take a moment to be grateful for that lesson.

Fall in Love with Your Scars

> Not only so, but we also glory in our sufferings, because we
> know that suffering produces perseverance; perseverance,
> character; and character, hope. And hope does not put us
> to shame, because God's love has been poured out into our
> hearts through the Holy Spirit, who has been given to us.
>
> ROMANS 5:3-5

have a scar on my knee. Every time I see it, I remember the story
of how it got there. I'm transported to the smell of grass and
mud and sweat. The sound of cleats and kicks, of classmates and
parents yelling from the stands . . . then the sudden stop of all the
sounds and the collective gasp when I fell. The blur of my coach and
our team's trainer surrounding me, helping me up, assuring me I'd
be okay. The injury that caused that scar also caused the end of my
soccer "career." Now, as you know, I just play for fun.

That's the thing about scars: they tell a story. And while it's a story
of pain, the middle and end of the story point to healing. Because the
healing process is what changes a wound to a scar. It's that way with
physical scars, but it's that way with spiritual and emotional scars too.

The hurt you experienced at church. (Been there.) When the friend
you thought was loyal betrayed you. (There too.) The breakup when

you thought it was going to last. (No thanks.) The unfulfilled dreams. (Why?) Job loss, a scary diagnosis, disappointment, miscarriage.

We have the option to shift our perspective from "scars are evidence of wounds" to "scars are evidence of healing." It's a slight shift when you see it on paper, but I know it's easier said than done. It takes hope that something good can come out of a circumstance that feels only bad. It takes opening up our hearts and our hands and our eyes to see if we can find the gifts in the healing.

A gift like unexpected strength. You get a few weeks, months, years down the road and look back and see a confidence and resolve in yourself that you didn't know you were capable of. Or a gift like empathy that enables you to see the difficulty others are walking through with a new level of compassion. And ultimately, healing gives the gift of hope. When you've been wounded and seen the way God heals, you have assurance that He can do it again and again. You know you're going to be okay.

CHASE THE FUN

Look for chances to show up with the strength, empathy, and hope you've gained from your scars.

Fall in Love with Hard Conversations

Let us therefore make every effort to do what leads to peace and to mutual edification.

ROMANS 14:19

I had a puppy for six days. It was a hard conversation, the one when I had to call and say that I couldn't keep her. See, even though Helen (that's what I named this fluff ball of a guardian angel cavapoo that God gave me for just under a week) was supposed to be hypoallergenic, no one seemed to have told my body about that, and I was for sure allergic to her. I hated having to say that she couldn't stay. It felt deeper than defeat and loss. It broke my heart. But it was the right conversation to have.

It was a hard conversation when I sat across from my pastor, Kevin Queen, while Helen slept in his lap, and processed why I had to have these particular hard conversations. What I was maybe getting to learn through them. What was on the other side of the hard conversations.

He said, "I think this is a test from God. Not for Him to see if you would pass, but for you to see if you could. Maybe you needed to know that you could love this much. Maybe you needed to see that you would be willing to sacrifice time and money and sleep for someone else that you love more than yourself." What he said wasn't hard because it was mean or hurtful but because it was true. It was so right, and it was pressing on a bruise I felt deep in my guts that, honestly, I needed to feel.

Having hard conversations is just that: hard. But what comes on the other side is almost always worth it. It's okay if it feels uncomfortable. It's smart to write out or rehearse what you want to say. It's wise to pray about the conversation and for the hearts of those involved. And it's faith to trust that there's something good on the other side of it.

That's why falling in love with hard conversations makes any sense at all. (And coming from your friend Annie F. Downs, the Enneagram type Seven who avoids tough emotions whenever possible, that's really saying something.)

CHASE THE FUN

Have you been avoiding a difficult conversation? If so, set it up. The good that comes on the other side is always worth it.

Fall in Love with Being Led

Submit to one another out of reverence for Christ.
EPHESIANS 5:21

The way to fall in love with being led is to start with choosing the right person to follow.

When your friend who's making dinner plans for the group is attuned to what's best for everyone, there's no stress in being along for the ride. You know she isn't going to choose a restaurant that exclusively serves shellfish that will LITERALLY kill Allison.

When your boss has integrity and humility, it's fun to sign on for challenging projects and to show up to work with enthusiasm for your role. You know you can trust her judgment and concern for the ultimate good of the team and the company.

When you and your spouse each put the other's needs first, it's a pleasure to submit to each other. (There, I said it. The "S" word. No, I'm not married yet and haven't done the whole mutual submission in marriage thing, but I hear it's a great way for things to work!) Even when the conclusion isn't what you initially wanted, you trust your spouse's opinions and know your best interests are highly valued by your partner.

Because Jesus is true and gracious and compassionate and faithful, following Him is the very best way to walk through life. You know that He will only lead you places that are part of His good plan for you.

I can almost hear the protests: "Yeah, but Annie, if you only knew what my boss was like . . ." If that's where you find yourself, there's still the chance to follow well in any ways that don't compromise your values. There may be a gift for you in it.

Maybe you're in the fortunate spot of getting to choose who leads you. I encourage you to choose as wisely as you can. Whether in friendships, jobs, or relationships, falling in love with being led starts with choosing who you're going to follow. And in case I haven't made it clear, you can never, ever go wrong following Jesus. He's the very best leader.

You know what else is incredible about being led? Your heart can be at rest in a way that's seldom possible otherwise. You can exhale and be still, knowing you're being taken care of. There's peace and fun in not pressuring yourself to be the one who always has to know best, make the final decision, and bear the burden of the outcomes. Let yourself be led.

CHASE THE FUN

If there's someone in your life who is leading you well, tell them how grateful you are.

Fall in Love with Laughter

A cheerful heart is good medicine,
but a crushed spirit dries up the bones.

PROVERBS 17:22

D o you remember that scene in the movie *Mary Poppins* when Mary, Bert, and the Banks children join Uncle Albert for a tea party on the ceiling? You're singing the song already, aren't you? "I love to laugh loud and long and clear!" The fuel for that amazing scene and its incredibly memorable song was laughter (and some movie magic).

One of my favorite things about laughing is how contagious it is. You know? Just try to keep a straight face when someone you're with belly laughs. Or try tickling your kiddo with a frown on your face. Or think of how a chuckle from a baby makes so many of us melt into laughter.

Best sound in the world? Children laughing. That was one of the most common answers whenever James Lipton asked that question during his *Inside the Actor's Studio* interviews. And one of the most common thoughts I have too. I think it's because of how pure and free and innocent laughter makes us feel.

Laughter lets off steam and relieves stress. Shared humor connects us with others. That's the beauty of a good inside joke.

Laughter forces us to breathe deeply, which is good for us both physically and emotionally. Even if you're a serious person. No matter if you're an introvert or an empath or have a highly philosophical personality. We all need a good laugh now and again. Maybe even more so if it's not something that comes naturally.

And particularly if you're going through some heavy circumstances or if you're dealing with major stress or a season of grief, laughter could be the medicine your heart needs. Seeking out (or even creating) moments of levity is not a betrayal (or numbing or escapism) of the tough thing and the serious processing it deserves. It's the balance you need, the medicine that helps you keep walking through it.

CHASE THE FUN

Listen to a comedy podcast or watch a comedy special on your favorite streaming platform. Laugh on purpose today!

Fall in Love with Cheering for Others

Correction does much, but encouragement does more.
JOHANN WOLFGANG VON GOETHE

There was a season a few years ago when I was really involved with the college ministry at my church, and the Lord saw fit for me to play the role of older sister to this amazing SQUAD of college guys. It just so happened that they were all on the baseball team at Vanderbilt University in Nashville. And I became a FAN FOR LIFE.

My friendships with these guys ignited in me a newfound joy in cheering other people on. When their season was going great, I felt like I'd maybe given them a little wind in their sails with all the yelling I was doing from the stands. And when things weren't going as well, I got to remind them of who they were and what really mattered and how resilient I knew them to be. It was so fun to get to do that while they were playing ball. It was even more fun (still is) to cheer for them off the field.

Even after they graduated and moved all over the country, we would read books together and talk about them. We'd pray together.

To this day, we grab dinner when I'm in their cities or they're in mine. And I get to put a little wind in their sails. Celebrate with them. Remind them of who they are.

It makes me think about what fun it is to celebrate people and to celebrate WITH them. See, there's a temptation for us to believe that, when people get things worth celebrating in their lives, there will be less to go around for us. Friends will sometimes ask me how I'm able to find joy when another person receives something I've been praying for in my own life. My response is this: that's THEIR answer to THEIR prayer. I'm not praying for someone else's opportunities. When my friend Emma got engaged to my other friend Eli, I was unconditionally over the moon for them. Because, as great as Eli is, I don't want to be engaged to Emma's future husband. I want to be engaged to MY future husband.

An amazingly fun thing about God is how limitless He is. How sufficient. He has more than enough blessing to go around. A better way to say it is that HE IS more than enough blessing to go around. He's more than enough for me. He's more than enough for you. So, fall in love with cheering people on. Keep confetti poppers at the ready! (You KNOW I do!)

CHASE THE FUN

Cheer someone on today.

Fall in Love with Someone

> But hope that is seen is no hope at all. Who hopes for what they already have?
>
> ROMANS 8:24

There are just so many myths out there about falling in love. They're in all the songs. The romantic comedies and the Hallmark movies we've been brought up on tell us that we can expect our lives to turn out the same way as the lives of these lovely leading ladies and handsome fellas.*

I want to believe that two people can find each other against all odds.

I want to believe that a spectacularly uncanny meet-cute is in my future.

I want to believe that when his mega-big-box book retailer threatens to run my local neighborhood bookshop out of business, true love will result from our email pen-pal relationship.

I want to believe in happy endings.

---

*Please don't hear me say that you shouldn't listen to love songs or watch romantic movies. By all means, do so if you enjoy them! I do! Just also tell yourself the truth and invite in wise counsel and be open to possibilities that don't fit into culturally prescribed narratives.

Maybe you do too? Or maybe you've been burned or disappointed in previous relationships? Or maybe you don't have much experience with the whole dating scene and it feels really scary?

Well, first of all, it IS scary. All new things are. And second, a lot of us are walking with the limp of disappointment that things have not or are not turning out the way we hoped they would. And third, we all want to believe in happy endings.

But who are we if not a brave group of friends who know how to look at something scary, remind ourselves we're not alone, and let ourselves be amateurs as we take courageous steps forward?

Maybe we just need to start by talking to God about our hopes. We can tell Him the type of person we're longing to meet. If I've learned nothing else in the last few months, I am confident of this: God hears us every time we pray. And He cares about the details of our lives.

And then maybe we need to listen to Him about how He sees us. This helps us remember what's true about us and about Him. Like the fact that we're made in His image, that He's always with us, that He has good plans for us. Remembering these truths helps us walk into new situations more confidently.

And last, let's say to Him and to ourselves, "I'm open to meeting someone today."

CHASE THE FUN

Look at yourself in the mirror and say out loud,
"I'm open to meeting someone today."

Fall in Love with Your Friends

> I cannot even imagine where I would be today were it not
> for that handful of friends who have given me a heart full of
> joy. Let's face it, friends make life a lot more fun.
>
> CHARLES R. SWINDOLL

never could have imagined or hoped for how things turned out the day I waited with friends outside the stage door of the Tennessee Performing Arts Center, where we were hoping to meet some cast members of *Wicked*. The story God decided to write is better than I could've dreamed up.

The show had been magical. I was enthralled—not just by the story and the talent but by the obvious chemistry and connection between the actors who played Glinda and Elphaba. So I made up my mind that I wanted to be friends with them. And because they're dear and fun and generous, Mary Kate and Ginna Claire opened up their little circle and snuggled me right in.

Since then, our lives have changed and we've each faced some big challenges and some heartbreaks and some amazing experiences and some dreams come true. And even though we don't live in the same cities and our jobs are really different and our backgrounds couldn't be more varied, we've walked through all of these circumstances TOGETHER.

Ginna Claire has this whimsical wonder and kindness about her. Mary Kate is spunky and honest. It's not hard to notice these things about them, because it's just who they are. And who they are makes me want to support and cheer for and love them well.

I try to notice such things about all my friends so I can shine a spotlight on them when they need a little encouragement. My friend Jenn takes caring about people in personalized detail to the level above next level. My friend Jon tells the truth in ways that make me think in new perspectives while also feeling known and understood and loved. My friend Kelley has unbridled, contagious enthusiasm that's generous and warm. My friends Annie and Dave are family to me (like, emergency-contact family), and Dave makes me laugh harder than most anyone on the planet.

Maybe your circle of friends is huge, or maybe it's small. Either way, notice the things that make your friends who they are. Fall in love with your friends. Cultivate your friendships with time and intention and follow-through and encouragement. Shine your spotlight on them, and let them know why they matter in your life.

CHASE THE FUN

Tell one of your friends why you appreciate them today. Maybe in a text, but maybe in a handwritten note, on the phone, or in person.

Fall in Love with Your Dreams

> When the LORD restored the fortunes of Zion,
>   we were like those who dreamed.
> Our mouths were filled with laughter,
>   our tongues with songs of joy.
>
> PSALM 126:1-2

On the surface, encouraging you to fall in love with your dreams feels a little unnecessary. If you didn't already love them, they wouldn't be your dreams. Whether it's your hope for a relationship or to become a parent, to start a nonprofit or to write a book, your dreams are part of your story's unique fingerprint on the world. And that really matters.

So, it's likely you already love your dreams. You spend time thinking about them. You rehearse scenarios and think through what-ifs. But the way to bring dreams into reality is to move past the first-date butterflies and go all in. Falling in love with your dreams is not a feeling. It's a commitment. It involves making choices and taking action. It involves risk and experimentation and permission to be an amateur, but also a level of grit and stick-to-itiveness.

Here are a couple of ideas that I think could help you:

Listen to advice, but not everyone's. Narrow down which voices get to speak into what you do with your dreams to a few wise people who have proved over time that they are FOR you and that they're willing to tell you the truth. People who are for you but are scared to tell you tough things are great encouragers to have around. You need them. But they tend to be "yes" people, so you also have to keep that in mind. People who will tell you tough things but aren't for you are the critics whose voices tend to be disproportionately loud in our lives. They may make you mad enough to fuel you for a little while, but it's not the kind of lasting fuel you need to pursue your dreams for the long haul.

Commit, but stay open-handed. God gives us our dreams or inspires them or opens doors for them. And if we trust Him to plant those dream-seeds in us, we must trust Him with how He grows them . . . or doesn't. Because He may close doors or reroute our paths. As shaky as it can feel when He does that and we don't understand why, our history with Him tells us we can stay open-handed with our dreams because He loves us and knows what's best for us.

So, fall in love with your dreams. And fall in love with the detours God takes you on as you commit to and pursue those dreams.

CHASE THE FUN

Take a step toward a dream today. It could be saying it out loud to someone, writing out a plan, or asking for wise counsel. Just take a step.

Fall in Love with Your City

> Also, seek the peace and prosperity of the city to which I have carried you into exile. Pray to the LORD for it, because if it prospers, you too will prosper.
>
> JEREMIAH 29:7

I remember when I decided I wasn't going to be leaving Nashville. The year I moved here, I pretty much counted down the days until I would be able to move away from here. I thought it would take a little time to get my career off the ground and then I would head back to my hometown in Georgia. My dentist was still there, a storage unit of my furniture was still there, my best friends and family were all still there too.

But then one random day, I started to wonder how different my life would be in Nashville if I didn't have an escape plan. If I brought up those last few boxes, found a new doctor and a new dentist, and invested in friendships like this would be where I lived out my days. What would change? Would my life and my experiences really be different if I fell in love with my city?

Yes, everything changed for me.

It really did. And yes, it really will for you too.

When you fall in love with your city—not just your street or your neighborhood but every corner of your city—your compassion increases. Your care and concern for your neighbors expand. You notice things—like a restaurant closing or a coffee shop opening. You notice which families are always at the park after grabbing some groceries from the farmers market, and you notice when your favorite associate no longer works at the local gift shop on the corner. You just see more when you are committed to a place.

The churches matter to you. Not just the one you attend but all of them. Because you love your city, you want to see it flourish. One of the things we talk about a lot in Nashville is that if everyone in our city who doesn't go to church decided to attend on a Sunday morning, there wouldn't be enough chairs for them in all the churches combined! So wouldn't we WANT every church to thrive?

And when you love your city, the poor and underprivileged matter more to you because you want everyone to thrive. So your decisions are different and how you serve is different because you love your city.

So enjoy the restaurants and the parks and the events. That will help you love where you live. But it's a deeper thing, a heart thing, a staying thing, that will make that commitment to love your city so worth it.

CHASE THE FUN

What do you love most about where you live?
Maybe today is a good day to go on another
walk around this place you call home, or to
try a new restaurant or visit a new shop.

Fall in Love with Your Story

> I am a little pencil in the hand of a writing God who is sending a love letter to the world.
>
> MOTHER TERESA

When I was a teacher, I got to teach my fifth graders a unit on the parts of a story. A good story has a beginning, middle, and end. But we all know it's more nuanced than that, right? There's the setting, the characters, the conflict, and the resolution.

Your story, the one you're living right now, has all those things too. Your life has a setting. The city you live in, the community, neighborhood, home you're nestled in, they have a character all their own, and they're basically characters in your story. Then there are the actual characters, your friends, family, coworkers, classmates. The people you get to interact with and influence and love and learn from. And I'm guessing, just based on the fact that you're a human living on planet earth, that your story's got some conflict.

It's funny how, even as fifth graders, we can comprehend and appreciate the fact that a good story doesn't just *have* conflict; it really *needs* conflict. That's how the characters become more dynamic, how they change and grow. That's why the story is interesting at all.

I mean, who wants to read *Pride and Prejudice* without all of the . . . well, pride and prejudice that go on between Elizabeth and Mr. Darcy? Not this girl! And what kind of ride is *You've Got Mail* if Kathleen Kelly and The Shop Around the Corner don't have to take a stand against the big, bad retailer Fox Books? A boring one, that's what.

Whether you're facing the "I don't have what I want yet so I'm trying to wait well" kind of conflict, or the "I work for a really challenging boss but I want to move forward in my career" kind of conflict, or the "I have a passion bigger than myself and I don't know what to do with it" kind of conflict (or any of the billions of other types), just know that those parts of the story exist for really good reasons. We can't always see it at the time, but the Author of your story has good plans for you. He created you ON purpose, FOR a purpose.

So you can fall in love with your story because you know and can trust the Author. He writes REALLY good stories. And He's writing one with you.

CHASE THE FUN

Make a list of the setting, key characters, and main conflicts in your story right now. Ask the Author to lead, guide, and bless you as He continues to write your story.

Fall in Love with Your Hobbies

A hobby a day keeps the doldrums away.
PHYLLIS MCGINLEY

When I meet new people, I often try to think of creative ways to skirt around those first few typical where-are-you-from-and-what-do-you-do questions. I mean, I DO like knowing where people are from because I inevitably have been there or know someone from there, and I love making connections like that. And it IS fun to know what people do for a living. That's one of the ways friends are helping to put the world back together, with the good work they do.

It's just that those aren't the ONLY things that matter about people, and there are some patterns and temptations in our society that make it easy to find our identity all wrapped up in what we do for work. I also don't want to make assumptions about people's lives. And there are LOTS of ways that people spend their time that they don't get paid for. Lots of really worthwhile and meaningful things. So, I enjoy asking people questions like "How do you spend your time?" and (wait for it . . .) "What sounds fun to you?" because their answers round out the picture of who they are and what matters to them.

Here's a little secret, one I'm trying to dispel the mystery around: what you do for fun MATTERS.

It doesn't just matter because it helps you connect with people. (Although it does.)

It doesn't just matter because it's good for your body and your mind. (Although it is.)

It doesn't just matter because it keeps you from scrolling mindlessly for hours. (SAY IT WITH ME: "Scrolling is not a hobby!")

What you do for fun matters because it helps your heart come alive and helps you be fully YOU. When you're fully YOU, you are a piece of Eden walking and talking and interacting in the world.

So fall in love with your hobbies. Don't just dabble. Spend the time. Buy the gear (when you've budgeted and it's responsible to do so). Invest in lessons. Tell people all about it. Invite others in. FALL IN LOVE with your hobbies and go all in!

CHASE THE FUN

Take one practical step toward falling in love
with one of your hobbies this week.

Fall in Love with Your Life

When it's over, I want to say: all my life
I was a bride married to amazement.

MARY OLIVER

The question people ask me maybe more than any other is this: "If you could give one piece of advice to your younger self [or to a twenty-year-old, thirty-year-old, or college student], what would it be?" Without hesitation, my answer is this: *fall in love with your life*.

Fall in love with your life. Fall in love with it as a college student. Fall in love with it as a twentysomething. Love it when you're thirty, fifty, eighty. Fall in love with single life, married life, mom life. Fall in love with your life.

See, there will always be things you *want*. And there will always be things that you *have*. In different seasons of your life, many of your wants will become things you have. The job, the relationship, the house, the security. And then you'll have new wants.

Sometimes the things you have will be exhausting or scary or uncomfortable. Like when it's time to take finals or when a tiny person has said your name four thousand times in five minutes. Sometimes they will be exhilarating and breathtaking. Like when you get to travel to the country you've always wanted to visit or say "I do" to the person you want to spend your life with.

Sometimes the things you want will break your heart or make you wait a really long time. Like the job opportunity you didn't get or the little blue lines that just wouldn't appear on that stick.

There will always be things you want and there will always be things you have.

With that truth as a baseline, we can still choose to love our lives. To look at the things we have as opportunities to be grateful and to create and steward and connect and love—what's more fun than that? And to look at the things we want as chances to hope, to trust God with His plans for our lives, to stay curious and keep wondering. That's fun too! I know it's a different kind of fun, but who says we can have only one kind?!

CHASE THE FUN

Make a list of things you have and things you want. Thank God for what you have and ask Him specifically for what you want (and for the strength to trust Him with the answers).

Fall in Love with Yourself

Oh, I'm so inadequate. And I love myself!

MEG RYAN

'm working on falling in love with myself. I know that may sound weird unless you love Lizzo like I do, and then you KNOW that you're your own soul mate. But for too long, I've decided that how I feel about me is based on how *you* feel about me. Or, more honestly, how *he* feels about me, whoever the current "he" is. The lack of love for myself has become somewhat toxic for me.

Not too long ago, I talked with a friend about how I am changing the way I view myself. See, those toxic insecurities—the false (but LOUD and kinda mean) stories I tell myself about why I should second-guess and who I should be more like—they are not problems that marriage or having a man in my life will fix. Because I know that my insecurities while trying to find a man will not disappear upon finding one; they will simply shape-shift. They may look like new iterations or sound like new questions, but they will be the same old toxins. New bottle, same poison.

The best way I know to fall in love with yourself is to say true things about yourself to yourself. Only you'll need to stay plugged in to a source of truth in order to have that steady flow of truth readily available at all times. That's why spending time reading the Bible is so crucial. It's the best way to stay plugged in to what God says about you, how He feels about you, what's true about you.

What He says about you is that you're a masterpiece. You're loved. He delights in you. You're forgiven. You're a work in progress. He has called you by name and you belong to Him. He has a plan for you (and it's good). You bear His image.

When we tell ourselves the truth, it becomes increasingly easier to believe that truth. Now, I'm not saying that we should flatter ourselves and pretend there aren't ways we need to change and grow. Imperfection is just part of being human. Acknowledging those imperfect parts of yourself (without piling on shame) and choosing to love yourself anyway, just like God does, is probably the most sacred work of falling in love with yourself. You may have to do that work a little bit every day—I know I do—but it will set you up beautifully to love God, others, and yourself from the very core of who you are. And that sounds FUN!

CHASE THE FUN

Tell yourself five true, good things about yourself.

Fall in Love with Fun

I never lose sight of the fact that just being is fun.
KATHARINE HEPBURN

You remember the scene in *The Sound of Music* when Fraulein Maria takes the von Trapp children gallivanting around the countryside in the play clothes she sewed for them out of old curtains? They sang, they picnicked, they went canoeing, they climbed trees. It was an experience in stark contrast to the rigid way their father typically ran the household. And you can tell. They're just so light, free, joyful, alive. How were those kid actors that good?!

I have a theory: it was the play clothes.

Play clothes. As a kid, even though I loved going to church (my friends were there, so of course I loved it! #AlwaysAnnie), I DID put up a bit of a fight on Sunday evenings when my mom would call me in from outside, tell me to change out of my play clothes, and we would head back for the Sunday evening service. Things are just better when you get to do them in your play clothes, right?

It's the freedom of "not real pants." (That's what I called them when I was tallying the days that I wore slippers or shoes and real pants or not real pants during quarantine in 2020.)

Play clothes give us the same things fun gives us. Feeling unencumbered, light, comfortable. Like we can move freely in the world and sit criss-cross-applesauce if we want. THAT'S what fun does for us. And it's why we need to carve out space and time for fun every day. It can be as simple as smiling and making eye contact with people. Spending time with friends. Getting outside. Maybe choosing a comedy podcast to listen to or a funny meme account to follow on social media. One of my friends posts amusing things that she finds on the internet as a little collection every Sunday, and I kid you not, I look forward to it every week and laugh out loud when I watch her stories.

Fun isn't frivolous or irresponsible. It's not immature or unproductive. It's good and kind and pure and needed. Fall in love with fun.

CHASE THE FUN

Look at your calendar and find the activity you're most looking forward to. Let yourself daydream about it for five minutes a day until the day arrives when you get to do it.

Would love to hear you talk about how hobbies are worship, because they can be in my opinion. | Jess

I don't even know where to start to find a hobby! Help! | Kayla

How do I find a sustainable hobby and not feel guilt when it doesn't serve me anymore? | Rebekah

Any tips for exploring new hobbies? | Lauren

How can I get into a hobby with friends? | Joy

Do hobbies vary by generations? | Sara

What's your best tip for finding time for fun with young kids? | Lauren

What's one tangible way to keep a hobby a hobby, not turning it into a job? | Kylie

What's the driving force behind the culture of joy and fun? | Hilary

FIND A HOBBY

What Is a Hobby?

> If you are losing your leisure, look out!—It may be you are losing your soul.
>
> LOGAN PEARSALL SMITH

My girlfriends and I piled into a booth at Virago, a bougie sushi restaurant in Nashville where I love to go for special occasions. There were eight of us in all. This particular occasion was a couple of weeks past my birthday, but since I'd been out of town on the actual day, this was my birthday girls night celebration. Our conversation was fast and meandering at the same time, but at some point I brought up the idea of hobbies. And I asked them if they had any hobbies.

In this group, we are mothers and wives and girlfriends and friends. We are employees and employers. We are homeowners and home renters. We are churchgoers and church skippers. But that question silenced all of us.

No one had an answer. No one had a hobby. It was like we all had forgotten that hobbies were an option, but when we started to think back—yeah, we wanted one.

Things came up that felt like they reminded us of Eden. Things like . . .

gardening

cooking

singing

fishing

By definition, hobbies are activities "done regularly in one's leisure time for pleasure."* Sounds pretty simple, right?

Done regularly means there's some rhythm to it. A hobby might not be an everyday aspect of life, but it's something you come back to.

In one's leisure time implies that we keep some part of our calendars and our hearts free and available to whimsy, to joy, to being intentionally unproductive.

For pleasure is simply permission to do something for the enjoyment of it. If it's fun for you, it's fun. Period. For some reason, I have to remind people of that quite often.

So, I'll ask you the same question I asked my friends around that table piled with edamame shells and sushi plates: Do you have a hobby? Something you do regularly in your leisure time for pleasure? If the answer is no, let's see if we can't figure out why. And better yet, let's see if we can't help you change that answer to a hearty yes!

CHASE THE FUN

What's your hobby?

*Lexico Oxford Dictionary, s.v. "hobby," accessed May 21, 2020, https://www.lexico.com /en/definition/hobby.

Why Do Hobbies Matter?

It is always the simple that produces the marvelous.

AMELIA BARR

My friend Laura said to me over apps and drinks at a happy hour not too long ago, "I think we are living in the hungriest generation ever." And I knew she wasn't just talking about food; she was talking about our souls. We fill our calendars and fill our lives and try to fill our bank accounts and our hearts. Something about that hunger prompted Laura to make a list of things she wanted to try.

As she thought out loud about those things, I listened and imagined and nodded. Everything she listed required her to be an amateur. Everything she listed required her to fall in love in one way or another. Everything she listed was an activity that you could call a hobby.

Laura wanted to make a list because she needs to create some space in her life, to have some new experiences, and (I think, deep down inside) to feed that hunger. Laura needed a hobby or two. I would actually say we all do.

Hobbies make space. They remind us of something beautiful and that good can come from nothing. That seeds become flowers and ingredients become soup and yarn becomes mittens. And when the whole world is broken, it's just nice to know we have the tiniest ability to put some pieces—even if they are actual, literal puzzle pieces—together, where they belong.

That's why hobbies matter. Because everything in our lives can't be only about producing, hustling, and striving. We need activities in our lives that exist for the pure enjoyment of doing them. Bit by bit, the things we do that bring us joy and God glory begin to draw a map back to Eden. To the wonder and peace, the deep sigh of rest, that come from allowing ourselves to simply exist with God.

CHASE THE FUN

Make a list like Laura's of things you want to try.

How Do I Find a Hobby?

Where you invest your love, you invest your life.

MUMFORD AND SONS

A s often as I think about fun, and as often as I'm sitting at a microphone in the *That Sounds Fun* podcast studio asking people what sounds fun to them, I wasn't aware so many people felt this lost when it comes to finding a hobby.

Why is that? As far as I can tell from my extensive research and accreditation as a Certified Fun Coach (I'm just kidding. That's not a thing. But I'm thinking of making it a thing!), there are a couple of hobby hurdles we need to jump before we find our hobbies.

The first hobby hurdle is *permission*. It's easy to convince ourselves that we're not allowed to spend any part of our limited time doing something that isn't productive. I hope the last couple of days (well, really the last 67 days) have helped you open up to the idea that hobbies matter. Leisure time matters. Enjoying your life matters. So, if you're having difficulty mustering up confidence that you are, in fact, the boss of your life, just go look at yourself in the mirror and say, "My friend Annie F. Downs says I have permission to find a hobby."

The other hobby hurdle is *embarrassment*. Friend, this space is like Planet Fitness—it's a judgment-free zone. If it's a hobby you want to try, you get to try. Period. It's fine if it's not for everyone. What if it's just for you? You deserve that.

Okay, now that we've jumped the hurdles, it's time to dig in. I talked with a reporter not too long ago who asked me this question about how to find a hobby, and I responded with some questions of my own. As we talked, I watched his buttoned-up, professional demeanor kind of melt into childlike, wistful wonder and then bubble over into a couple of tears in the corners of his intuitive brown eyes. Here's what I asked him:

- What did you like to do on a free Saturday or after school when you were around nine or ten years old?
- When you were growing up, how did your family enjoy spending time together, especially time with grandparents or extended family?

You find a hobby by giving yourself permission to try things that sound fun to you and that remind you of who you are or of a more carefree time in your life. It's that easy (AND that hard).

Chase the Fun

Answer those two questions for yourself, either out loud to a trusted friend or privately in your journal.

Hobbies Help You Learn

> The hallmark of successful people is that they are always
> stretching themselves to learn new things.
>
> CAROL S. DWECK

D id you ever read the darling children's book *The Very Hungry Caterpillar* by Eric Carle? It's the one where the caterpillar eats its way through fruits and veggies as readers get to see the vibrant colors and count the delicious foods. On one day the caterpillar even overindulges in too many sweets and savories and ends up with a stomachache. After it is done eating, though, it grows and changes and becomes what it was created to be: a beautiful butterfly. That caterpillar is what I think of when I try to imagine what curiosity looks like.

Curiosity is hungry. And when you feed it good things, it grows. It wants more, asks new questions, follows rabbit trails, leads to new wonderings and wanderings. As it grows, it changes and eventually transforms into something beautiful. It's the process of learning. And hobbies help you learn.

On the surface, curiosity in a hobby like knitting will help you learn different types of stitches. As you learn, you grow from knitting something with only straight edges, like a scarf, to something a little more intricate and complex, like a hat. What you learn on a deeper level, though, is that the stillness and focus of knitting enable you to process and let go of some anxiety you've been feeling.

When you take up tennis with the neighborhood league, you learn about different grips and swings and strokes and how to anticipate with your footwork. But you also discover leadership and connection skills that you never knew you had as you rise to the occasion of organizing and rallying the teams on the court each week.

Maybe it's baking that you devote some time to. That internet deep dive and a couple of experiments yield knowledge about which type of flour will rise just right and why using a kitchen scale works better than measuring cups for dry ingredients. But you also learn how it feels to have something homemade and warm to offer a new neighbor who moved in across the way, a level of hospitality and satisfaction that you've been craving but haven't quite known how to fulfill.

See, hobbies help you learn things. Facts, sure, and new skills, but also new ways to connect with yourself and to make space to process and rest. Hobbies teach you what makes you smile, what makes you frustrated, what makes you motivated to try again.

CHASE THE FUN

Think of something you're curious about.
Ask questions and search out the answers!
See where your curiosity leads.

Hobbies Help You Laugh

A day without laughter is a day wasted.

CHARLIE CHAPLIN

When I was an elementary school teacher, my fifth-grade students and I would spend time every Friday morning discussing a joke. Though it was important to me that they learn critical reading skills and were on track to meet their math benchmarks, I could NOT forgive myself if they didn't master other life skills before they headed off to middle school. Understanding why a joke is funny was one such skill.

The anatomy of a joke—the setup, the delivery, the punch line, the timing, the puns and wordplay. I just couldn't get enough of seeing the light bulbs go on for them and watching my sweet, twiggy, red-cheeked-from-running-races-on-the-playground eleven-year-olds throw their heads back in laughter because they REALLY GOT IT.

You know what else is funny? Trying something new. Being an amateur at it. Finding out the only way to get good at it will look somewhat clumsy at first. Deciding the stakes are low and the potential joy is high, so it's worth it. Laughing at (with) yourself because learning a new hobby is FUN. We need to give ourselves a pass to laugh with ourselves instead of immediately jumping to frustration or self-deprecation.

You know the best way to laugh? WITH people. Hobbies gather people around common interests. One of my very favorite things is going to a live concert or theater production with friends. Inevitably, one of the best moments of the evening is the chatter walking back to wherever the car is parked, when everyone is sharing their favorite moment from the show, and the enthusiasm escalates and everyone's talking over each other because there was so much to love about the experience. By the time we get back to the car, our sides ache from laughing.

You know one of the best kinds of jokes? Inside jokes. The ones that develop organically from that silly moment with your golf buddies when someone shanks a drive and someone else drops the perfectly timed one-liner from the cart. And then it gets repeated. And you can't even explain why it's so funny and do it justice. "You just had to be there . . ."

Since hobbies create connection and community and questions and opportunities NOT to be an expert, they also invariably create chances to laugh until your cheeks hurt. Take those chances any time they present themselves!

CHASE THE FUN

Tell someone the story of the last time you laughed really hard. What made the moment so funny? (You can totally tell me on social media—I'm @anniefdowns. And you KNOW I love these stories!)

Hobbies Help You Read More

Once you learn to read, you will be forever free.
FREDERICK DOUGLASS

You know what you can learn about in a book? No, it's not a trick question. You can learn literally ANYTHING. The problem isn't a lack of access to immense amounts of knowledge. The problem is when we stop wondering. When we stop being curious about and interested in new things, or about getting better at old things.

But hobbies ignite curiosity. They breed wonder. And not just the awe type of wonder but the question-asking type of wonder that inspires creativity and risk-taking. And it's ACTIVE. It makes us move.

Curiosity causes us to think, "I love playing golf. I have so much fun doing it. I wonder how I can learn to hit the ball farther or straighter?" or "What are the most popular courses of all time?" or "What have the best golfers in history learned through their years of playing?" A simple Google search, a trip to the library, or a look-see around a bookstore will yield countless options that can satiate that thirst to know more. From technical knowledge that will help you tweak your swing to inspiring stories of the greats that will tie your heart more closely to the game, reading about your hobbies is a great way to enjoy them even more.

Blogs are a fantastic place to read about cooking and baking, and you're all but guaranteed to also see gorgeous photographs of the recipe in progress—which, I must say, are very helpful to know if I'm on the right track when I attempt it! (HASHTAG FOOD BLOGGER ALERT) There are entire magazines about hunting and cross-stitching. (Not at the same time . . . although the intersection of those two hobbies would be interesting!) There's so much good stuff out there to read that will enhance how you enjoy your free time.

And it probably goes without saying, but as your friend who's done a lot of research on hobbies and leisure time and fun, I should point out that one hobby that shows up on all the lists of popular hobbies is reading itself. Now, I know I'm an author and also an avid reader, so I'm acknowledging that I'm ENTIRELY biased about this, but reading is seriously one of the best hobbies.

Find a list of classics and read your way through them. Read a poem a day. Read a book a month, alternating between fiction and nonfiction. Choose an author and read through their entire body of work. Join a book club, which has a bonus: variety, conversation, and connection!

CHASE THE FUN

Read up on one of your hobbies. If you're not sure where to start, just type a simple question into the Google search bar and follow the rabbit trail!

Hobbies Help You Understand Seasons

There is a time for everything,
and a season for every activity under the
heavens.

ECCLESIASTES 3:1

My book club in Georgia was full of women I had known my whole life; my Nashville book club was swimming with strangers. I had never seen most of the faces before that first night in August when we sat outside on a porch and talked about a book we had all devoured. I couldn't believe I was already in some sort of group. I had lived in Nashville for only a few weeks and here was a collection of women making space for me when they gathered around a story.

As the months and years passed, that book club was a constant. I got to host a few times, and the first time I did, I dove back into the book club folder in my mind and knew I needed a recipe from the book. So I called our favorite local bakery and got a cake made, just like the one in the book. It had real flowers as decorations and everything. I wasn't the guest; I was the host. I wasn't the new girl;

I was welcoming the new girl who had just moved to town. I wasn't the youngest in the room; I was the thirtysomething woman hosting in my home, candles lit and beautiful plates out on the table. The throw pillows on the couch were fluffed, and I wasn't rushed before the women arrived. I had become the women I watched and admired a decade before, in a different city and a different time.

I didn't know hobbies did that, but this one did. The longer I practiced this hobby, the more I saw myself becoming who I wanted to be. Not only were my hosting skills improving, but I was also reading so much. I was being stretched and taught by the books and the women who sat with me and talked about what we read.

Isn't that the way seasons pass? Gradually, naturally, in due time, but then you look up and all of a sudden summer heat has given way to the colors of fall.

Some hobbies, like a book club, serve you throughout changing seasons. And some are more seasonal and dependent on the rhythms of nature, like gardening or swim team. Still others shine a light on life seasons that are short-lived, like mommy-and-me gymnastics or a seniors bridge club. All of them, though, help us understand the seasons we're walking through, because they help us understand ourselves.

CHASE THE FUN

Take inventory of what you like to do in your free time during each season: winter, spring, summer, and fall.

Hobbies Help You Heal

This hope is a strong and trustworthy anchor for our souls.
It leads us through the curtain into God's inner sanctuary.

HEBREWS 6:19 NLT

A ndy decided to become a Little League coach because he loves baseball. The smell of the freshly cut grass. The crack of the bat and the hum of the lights. The strategy and the teamwork. The connection between the pitcher and catcher. The sunflower seeds and the dugout energy. Every single detail transcends time and space for him.

Baseball transports Andy to a simpler time. A time when his dad was his third base coach, and he was so tuned in to the voice and directions of his father that every other sound faded away. To endless evenings of throwing the ball around in the backyard with his dad as the fireflies came out to play too.

It's been six years since Andy's dad passed away. The grief comes in waves, but his father is alive in Andy every time he shows a nine-year-old boy how to adjust his grip to get a better handle on the bat. Patient strength and quiet resolve are things he learned by example. And each time he gathers his team in the outfield to celebrate their successes, learn from their errors, hand out a game ball, and send the boys scuffling off to the concession stand for Icees, it's a way for his heart to heal a little more from the grief he carries. It lets him stay connected to memories that remind him who he is, where he came from, and who he wants to be.

Any time we spend on something that reminds us who we are and the type of person we want to be is time well spent. That's how we heal from the broken things in the world and the hard parts of our lives—by staying tethered to who God created us to be, trusting that He's still putting us back together.

We don't use our hobbies to stuff or numb or escape tough things. Instead, we let them provide space and time for us to process, to feel, to lament, and to find moments of levity so we can keep moving forward. Hobbies are such powerful tools for healing.

CHASE THE FUN

What do you do that helps you process
and heal from tough situations?

Hobbies Help You Rest

Truly my soul finds rest in God.
PSALM 62:1

My friend Tim has ALS. It's a terrible disease that has radically changed his life over the past few years. Because of ALS, everything in our current friendship is a bit slower. When I ask Tim a question, I then sit in the chair across from him and wait as he looks from letter to letter, typing words into a sentence with his eyes, and then after a few seconds, his incredibly smart computer speaks the words he's typed out loud.

I don't remember how it started, but one day Tim decided that he would teach me how to play chess. It always felt like a game that was out of my reach mentally, but Tim promised he'd be able to teach me and that it would even be fun. It also gave us a thing, you know? A thing we did that was an easy connection point, something intentional that didn't revolve around eating or drinking or doing anything active.

CHESS IS VERY HARD TO PLAY. But Tim, who is very good at chess, is also very good at being a patient teacher. And I have the added benefit of not only making my own moves but also following

Tim's directions to move his pieces. It's an interesting way to learn, playing from both sides.

I tend to run my life, and my fun, at an incredibly fast pace. Hurry to this, buzz through that, finish this thing so you can get to THAT. The slow pace of the game, the quiet of the room while one of us thinks through the next move, has not only slowed me down but also slowly softened something in me. I come to rest while we play. I feel the muscles in my face and neck relax. I start to notice things around the room and outside that I haven't seen before. As I'm sitting and waiting for Tim's move, studying the board, studying my friend, studying the breeze in the trees by the pool, I'm learning to rest in the fun.

And you can too. Choose a hobby that allows you space for what the other parts of your life don't. If your work involves a lot of interaction and extroversion, maybe a quiet hobby like doing puzzles will bring you rest. If your daily life demands hours of sitting at a desk staring at a computer, then a hiking club at your nearby park sounds like a fun respite to me.

CHASE THE FUN

Choose an activity this week that allows you to rest from the typical speed of your life. What makes you slow down your pace just a bit (or a lot)?

Hobbies Grow Your Walk with God

Peace I leave with you; my peace I give you. I do not give to you as the world gives. Do not let your hearts be troubled and do not be afraid.

JOHN 14:27

The world tells us a lot of things that aren't exactly true about what really matters and what boxes to check that add up to success. It tells us to hustle. It tells us that we must show up early and stay late and sacrifice our health and our sanity. We've got to be the best and the most put together and the most accomplished. (And don't get me wrong, "Work Hard" is posted on the wall at my office. It's a value I hold. I just hold it next to other values, like "Pray Hard. Rest Hard. Play Hard.")

But Jesus says we get peace a different way than what the world tells us.

There's peace that comes from spending time doing something that fills us up. There's peace that comes from assigning sections of our calendar to enjoyment and connection and community and rest.

People say all the time that we simply need to love God and love people. When I look at the Scripture passage where they find that idea, I see Jesus saying to love God with all our heart, soul, mind, and strength, and to love our neighbor as ourselves (Luke 10:27). That little detail that how we love ourselves informs how we love others is often overlooked. And I think it really matters.

We need to be kind to ourselves the way God is kind to us, and that gives us an overflow that we can love others out of.

If we're going to love God with all that we are—heart, soul, mind, and strength—then our calendars get to include sections of time that make way for joy and peace and love.

Your hobbies are soul work. When you laugh with the other members of your recreational kickball team, that's a piece of heaven come to earth. When you sit still and do a puzzle while listening to music, your heart is open to resting. When you finish a run as the sun rises, your strength is being renewed in that moment. When you have a lively conversation about a new book at book club, your mind is alive, and that brings glory to God.

If it's true that we are to love God and to love others as we love ourselves, then this pursuit of pleasurable activities to enjoy in our leisure time? It's holy. Your hobbies grow your walk with God.

CHASE THE FUN

Write down one way you've felt connected to God through a hobby. Why do you think it felt that way?

Hobbies Help You Grieve

Even in laughter the heart may ache,
and rejoicing may end in grief.
PROVERBS 14:13

I heard a story recently about a sweet family whose grandmother had passed away. It's a pain and loss that many of us have experienced and can empathize with; it is also deeply unique and can feel really isolating. Because no one else has *your* memories with *your* grandma, *your* shared experiences and knowing looks, the smells and the tastes of her homecooked meals . . . no one else has those, so the grief is heavy because it's only yours to carry.

That was especially true for the little five-year-old girl in this family. The depth of her bond with her grandmother transcended what ought to have been possible in five short years. And she was having a particularly difficult time processing where her grandmother had gone. Why she wasn't coming back. And really just how hard it was not to get to see her, hear her laugh, sit in her lap, and simply be with her anymore. It was the first time she'd encountered this type of loss.

To help the girl express her big feelings, even though they were unfamiliar and difficult, her mom did something I think is so brilliant. She went to one of her hobbies for help. Taking a shirt from this beloved grandmother's closet and utilizing the skills that her sewing hobby provided, she created a pillow encased in the shirt. Then, whenever this sweet girl was feeling like she "super missed" her grandma (her words—I know, so sweet), she would have this pillow to hug that looked like and smelled like and felt like her grandma.

All hobbies create space—to breathe, to discharge energy, to not think about anything else, to connect with our bodies. Some creative hobbies, like writing, painting, sculpting, and songwriting, provide space to process emotions. Other community-oriented activities, like book clubs and golf, give opportunities for supportive conversations. Seasonal, nature-related hobbies help us feel grounded and remind us of the ebbs and flows, the ups and downs, the cycles of life that give way to one another.

Grief is one of the most sacred, profound experiences we share as humans . . . if we let it be. It tells us that something or someone mattered to us deeply. And hobbies can help us walk through grief and receive all it has to teach us.

CHASE THE FUN

Are you grieving today? Spend some time on your hobby to create space for your grief.

Hobbies Help You Grow

Instead, we will speak the truth in love, growing in every way more and more like Christ, who is the head of his body, the church. He makes the whole body fit together perfectly. As each part does its own special work, it helps the other parts grow, so that the whole body is healthy and growing and full of love.

EPHESIANS 4:15-16 NLT

It's been years since I've had a traditional book club in my life. But that's because I've started something new. It's very small and sweet, but I'm telling you, it's just like a book club. It's only three of us, it's over lunch, and it's every other month. The pressure is low and the commitment is even lower, but we really care. We are reading works that are hard to read: things about racial injustice and the mistreatment of our environment. We are reading books by authors who aren't the same race as we are or in the same phase of life. We are reading fiction and nonfiction, but we're reading with purpose.

And it's another level of interesting and intentional and fun. It's a different thing. I have long passed grown-up status, but I continue to refine and make it better. This book club doesn't show me grown-ups. It doesn't make me feel like a grown-up. It's proof that I am a grown-up and proof that I'm working to be better.

I hope this book club will last. I hope this one has some distance to it. But maybe one of the things I love about a book club is it isn't forever. I never knew it wasn't, but now I do. And when you learn that, you love it differently. So I'm loving this book club differently.

It's a hobby that's growing me, and maybe, just maybe, reading books and talking about them will put the world back together in some little way. Or, at least, it will give me the words to try to teach myself how to do it.

Maybe hobbies are also moments along your path that tell you who you were and who you are and who you want to be. Maybe you're like me and they mark growth within yourself and your community and with God.

CHASE THE FUN

What are some specific ways your
hobbies have helped you grow?

Hobbies Help You Escape

> You will have to experiment and try things out for yourself and you will not be sure of what you are doing. That's all right, you are feeling your way into the thing.
>
> EMILY CARR

When I go hiking at Radnor Lake, one of my favorite hobbies, this thing happens. Really it happens whenever I spend time in motion outdoors. It's like all the automobiles that are zipping around in my mind, changing lanes and entering and exiting the freeway, get lined up in a row and start driving at the same speed and things just make sense. Somehow, having to focus on where my feet will land so that my toe doesn't catch on a root and needing to pay attention to my breathing provide this sense of escape.

Now, don't hear what I'm not saying. (I love that line. Pastor Kevin uses it when he preaches, and it gets me every time.) I am not encouraging you to escape your life—to rely on any numbing or self-medicating habits. I am not encouraging you to run from difficult emotions or to avoid making space for processing. What I AM saying is that sometimes hobbies provide the escape you need—in the form of space, time, enjoyment, movement, a brain break, or a breath of fresh air—that enables you to come back to "real life" with fresh energy and perspective.

I heard this same idea from two friends in one week, and it made me pause and take notice. One said the reason she loves cross-stitching is that it occupies her hands and her mind at the same time. It requires the type of focus that drowns out anything else, and yet it feels restful because she's so still while she's stitching. Since she picked it up as a hobby several months ago, she's seen a marked decrease in the effects of anxiety in her life.

Another friend, an avid golfer, was telling me why golf is such a lifeline for him. He has a fast-paced, high-pressure job, and then, you know, a life outside of that too. When he's on the golf course, his brain is maxed out with club choice and distance to the hole and wind speed, and it's basically the only time he takes a mental break from the demands that fill his life.

That's one of the gifts that hobbies give us. It's similar to the type of escape that a good vacation provides. Not because you want to get away from your life but because you want to get back to your life well rested, having gained perspective and being a more peaceful version of yourself.

CHASE THE FUN

Take a break. Escape to something fun. Take note of how you feel when you re-engage with "real life."

Hobbies Teach You Something New

We keep moving forward, opening new doors, and doing new things, because we're curious and curiosity keeps leading us down new paths.

WALT DISNEY

You may know this about me, because I've shared it on the podcast and I'm sure in other places as well, but I AM A SUCKER for the Wild West. Get me to Lost Valley Ranch and let there be horses and steers and ranch hands and an expanse of sky and rolling hills and scrubby shrubs.

It transports me to a bygone era of exploration and legend, and I just love stories that have a pioneering spirit in them. There's just something about the tenacity and courage it takes to venture into somewhere unknown and unexplored and to see what comes of it. That's what a hobby is! A great undiscovered territory to explore and expand into.

And the great thing about giving ourselves a pass to be an amateur is that there's so much out there we have yet to learn. Libraries exist for just such a reason. And YouTube is a veritable smorgasbord of how-to videos. For that matter, you can subscribe to MasterClass and be taught all KINDS of skills and hobbies by experts in the field. I adore the idea of learning from people who are passionate and committed and have put in the time and effort to become excellent at something. Want to learn beginning piano from a member of the orchestra or receive baking instruction from an award-winning chef? Technology makes learning new things so very accessible.

But hobbies don't just teach us skills. They also teach us about ourselves and the kind of people we want to be. Because our hobbies invite us into new disciplines and perseverance and victories and re-boots, they deepen our character. The joy and peace and connection we find through our hobbies enlighten us to ways our hearts can be formed and can invite others into flourishing.

As you continue on your path into unexplored territory, keep your eyes open and your head lifted for the tiny and significant (and in-between) discoveries you'll make along the way.

CHASE THE FUN

Ask a question related to one of your
hobbies and dig for the answer.

Hobbies Create Something New

True happiness comes from the joy of deeds well done, the zest of creating things new.

ANTOINE DE SAINT-EXUPÉRY

The secret sauce of my podcast is when I kind of forget there's a microphone and can pretend that my guest and I are just two people sitting at coffee trying to get to know each other or, if we are already friends, just having a convo to catch up.

In the process of getting to know Melissa d'Arabian, an amazing chef and Food Network star, I listened as she talked about beef stew. Her mother-in-law taught her an intricate and time-consuming recipe for the most delicious beef stew she had ever eaten, but it wasn't fast. Each ingredient had to be handled separately and purposefully. It is one of those recipes that could take most of your day, but the payoff is an insanely delicious and layered experience.

I'm a person who wants to enjoy the experience of eating as much as I enjoy the food. I like fancy restaurants not because I am bougie (okay, not ONLY because I'm bougie) but because of how they've thought through the entire experience the guest is going to have.

But the experience of cooking a meal is often more enjoyable than the eating of it. Cooking is medicine, right? (We talked about it on day 35. ☺)

That's how hobbies work. The making of the thing is just as rewarding, if not more so, than the actual product. I think back to times when women held quilting bees. They would sit around working on a quilt, talking, laughing, and sewing. The finished quilts were necessary and important for whoever received them, but the really good stuff was what happened around that circle.

The things hobbies create don't have to be physical, tangible things . . . though they can be. A work of art, a meal, an embroidered sweatshirt. Hobbies also create communities, inside jokes, experiences, memories, connections. New relationships, new food, new adventures. Sounds like Eden, doesn't it?

CHASE THE FUN

Choose a recipe you've never made and make it!

Hobbies Create Things for Others

> Remember that when you leave this earth, you can take nothing that you have received but only what you have given; a full heart enriched by honest service, love, sacrifice, and courage.
>
> FRANCIS OF ASSISI

During the months of 2020 that were characterized by COVID-induced quarantine and safer-at-home orders, I took up a couple of different hobbies. I know a lot of people did, either to maximize their extra time at home or to keep themselves from going crazy. One of the hobbies that I tried out was cross-stitching. Let me tell you, once I started, I could NOT put it down!

I enjoyed that I could turn on a great audiobook or even a mindless TV show or movie and also have something to do with my hands. Even more than that, cross-stitching seemed to fill this nostalgic gap, connecting me to a pace and an ease that felt as if I was sitting on my grandmother's sofa and sipping tea with her by lamplight. She is, after all, the reason I even knew about cross-stitching to begin with.

But the thing that sent my love for cross-stitching over the edge was the moment I found a darling pattern I fell in love with, and it was the perfect size for a Christmas ornament. Not only that, but if I budgeted my evenings and free time just right (I mean, where was I going? The whole world was locked down!), I could make enough of them to gift to my siblings and cousins for Christmas (and still have one for my own tree).

There was something so special about knowing that each year, when they lug their boxes and bins of holiday decorations down from the attic or out of the back of the guest room closet, and when they carefully unwrap their ornaments and hang them up, this gift, hand-made with love, will be a part of their tradition. The fact that matching ornaments will hang on all our trees is a connection that transcends distance and feels like the very best kind of tether to family.

See, hobbies don't just create something new; they create things for others. Baking warm cookies creates a welcome for new neighbors. Gardening creates bounty to share with friends and family. Kickball leagues create space for connection with friends new to town. Painting or writing or singing creates something beautiful that others can revel in. When we create for others, we're doing some of the work of putting the world back together again, even if it's in a small way. It's a way we get to partner with the Lord in all that Eden-bringing redemption work He's doing.

CHASE THE FUN

Decide what you'd like to create for someone else and mark off time on your calendar to do it!

Hobbies Help You Make Friends

Friendship . . . is born at the moment when one man says to
another "What! You too? I thought that no one but myself . . ."

C. S. LEWIS

A few years ago, eight o'clock on Sunday nights would find me
at Rocketown, a skate park and concert venue in Nashville
that my church used for a couple of hours each week to
host a service for college students. (And serve them cereal. Everyone
knows the way to college kids' hearts is free food!) One of those
nights, in walked this crew of TALL, muscle-y boys . . . men . . . maybe
somewhere in the middle of the two? These guys, who I would affec-
tionately refer to as my VandyBoys, were all on the baseball team at
Vanderbilt University, and they ended up becoming some of my very
best friends. Men who have let me in as a big-sister voice in their
lives and who have shared with me so many ups and downs, seasons
and celebrations.

And it wasn't just the students who captured my heart on those
Sunday nights. I went in DEEP with the other volunteers who couldn't
get enough of watching God change college kids' hearts and light

them on fire. Gosh. Those were fun nights, made so by the people I got to be a part of them WITH.

Now, this is not your friend Annie tooting her own horn. *Yeah, yeah, Annie. We get it. You love to serve at church.* No humble brags here. It's just my story. It's just the truth that some of the hobbies that have led to lasting friendships that are truly precious to me have centered around serving in my local church. And I think that could be true for you too. There's something powerful about the bonds that form from our common interests and the fun we have in these environments because they are built on a foundation of deeply rooted, shared relationships with the Lord.

But volunteer work in other arenas—like with Young Life, coaching sports, serving at a homeless shelter, or in the library at your kids' school—opens up similar opportunities to meet people you have things in common with (not the least of which is the activity at hand). Activities tend to attract like-minded and like-hearted people! It's that simple: hobbies help you make friends.

CHASE THE FUN

Introduce yourself to someone at church or at the place where you volunteer. And if you don't serve at church or volunteer somewhere, move "Find a Place to Volunteer" to the top of your hobby to-do list!

Hobbies Bring Friends Together

> Friends love through all kinds of weather,
> and families stick together in all kinds of trouble.
> PROVERBS 17:17 MSG

You want to come over and go fishing? A bunch of people are coming."

It's not the invitation I get MOST often on a spring evening, but something about it piqued my interest. "Yes?" I responded a little hesitantly but without really asking any more questions. The invitation came from my fellow Enneagram Seven friend Drew, and I'm crazy about his family and trust his sense of what a good time looks like.

Fishing: that sounds fun. It sounds nostalgic and dreamy and like something I would've done as a kid with my grandpa and cousins (never mind the worms and dirt and taking hooks out of fish mouths).

As I walked out to the pond at the front of Drew's neighborhood, with the slightly overgrown grass tickling my sandaled ankles, what I saw took my breath away. Because the mix of kiddos running around with potentially dangerous fishing poles over their shoulders was the perfect Venn diagram of my life.

Drew's three-year-old twins were trailed by his tween girls as sweet caregivers so their dad could have a chance to cast a couple of times. Drew's son AJ and his neighbor buddy immediately welcomed me into their football tossing triangle. Football and fishing . . . it was almost too deliciously Southern. I thought my heart might burst. We belonged in a country song.

The sun was setting, the mosquitoes and fish were biting, and my heart was busy being present in the moment and also trying to store it up for later. It was such a sweet surprise to show up not knowing exactly who or what to expect and being greeted with the comfort of friends I could exhale and be fully myself with.

Hobbies have this superpower to bring friends together. It can be old friends gathering over a newly discovered, shared enjoyment (for us that night, it was fishing). Or it can be friends you've just met, connecting because pickleball or craft brewing or songwriting are all things that are better explored with a community. Old or new, lasting or seasonal, let the friends your hobbies bring you and the hobbies your friends bring you be part of the rich way you chase the fun.

CHASE THE FUN

Ask someone to join you the next time you head out (or stay in) to participate in your hobby.

Hobbies Remind You of Family

You don't choose your family. They are God's gift to you, as you are to them.

DESMOND TUTU

One aspect of any cooking endeavor that brings me the most simple joy is visiting my local farmers market to load up on veggies. Something about strolling through stands and tents and folding tables covered in baskets and crates full of homegrown produce just slows me down in the best way. Knowing the farms and seeing the people who had a hand in growing the food I'm going to eat makes me feel grounded and connected, and I love it so much.

More than that, though, is the connection I feel to my grandmother and my mom when I'm there. Oh, the number of times that kid Annie, without a care in the world, ambled around a farmers market with one of these women. We would sample strawberries and thump melons and always bring home a basket or bag full of snap beans.

Then we would sit on the front porch of my grandmother's house during the coolest part of the day (which I can assure you was still blazing hot, because that's what Georgia summer days feel like), and we would snap those beans. Each into our own colander.

When I snap beans these days, it's rarely without a momentary smile for all the times that comfortable silence passed between the women in my family on that front porch of my grandparents' house on Ebenezer Road.

For me, it's snapping green beans. Maybe for you it's playing Scrabble or Yahtzee like you used to do with your aunts and cousins. Fishing like you did with your grandpa. Or following your team through every game, home and away, like you did with your dad as a kid.

Hobbies can be new and novel, but often they're born in us and grow with us from our families. And because they help us remember who we come from and where we come from, they also help us discover who we are and where we want to go.

CHASE THE FUN

Write down or share the stories or memories of your grandmother (or another relative) that come to mind when you're doing what you do for fun.

Hobbies Bring Families Together

Every chess master was once a beginner.
IRVING CHERNEV

One Christmas we got my dad a really nice chess set. Turns out (though I'd never really paid attention to this detail) my dad loves to play chess. It was a hobby of his as a child and teenager. He used to read books about chess and play it often.

He was excited—we could tell as soon as he opened the box—and it wasn't long before the pieces were set up.

I immediately offered to jump into a game. I figured it would be fun to use the skills I had gained from being clobbered by Tim to play with my dad. I was surprisingly nervous because it felt like meeting a side of him I didn't already know.

Being a grown-up with parents can set up weird moments like this, where you realize for the first time that your parents, while raising you, were just normal adults. It's kind of trippy, honestly. And then moments like this chess game happen, and not only do I feel I have a glimpse of my dad as a fellow adult, but I also feel like an adult seeing my dad as a child. Knowing what I know now, as an adult who relates to children, after learning about a part of my dad's childhood life, gives me a new view of him.

I played my dad that day and he obliterated me. I mean, I can't overstate how quickly and completely he destroyed me. And then he kindly smiled and asked if I wanted to set up the board and go again. And of course I did.

I knew the chances of ever beating him were slim, but I knew the chances of being with him were really high if I said yes again. I like playing chess . . . it's fun and all, but it mainly makes space for connection and time. Fun often breeds that. There's something specifically good and maybe holy about the way that our hobbies can slow us down and stretch out time with our people.

So dig for and excavate the things that you and your family want to gather around. Singing around grandma's baby grand, fishing in the pond at the back of the property, doing puzzles, playing card games, going to the theater to see ALL the musicals that come to your town, following your favorite team, cooking together . . . all of these are fun hobbies. But they're more profoundly fun when they're enjoyed with family.

CHASE THE FUN

Do something fun with a member of your family.

Hobbies Connect Us with Children

Play is the highest form of research.

ALBERT EINSTEIN

Annie! Come on!" An invitation like this from one of my mini-BFFs is seriously one of the sweetest sounds in the entire world to me.

See, I have this group of friends. A village. I guess *family* is the right word to describe our crew. (They're the emergency contacts on my official forms, so yes, I do think the term *family* applies.) And one of the aspects I specifically shine at in this family is I show up after a day of sitting at my desk working, after their mom has been with them doing the mom things all day, and I have fresh energy. I'm ready.

So, when they tell me to come on, I do! Sometimes it's to a particularly elaborate Lego build. And I get to sit down with the little booklet that came with the set and maybe help them back up a few steps, undo what needs to be undone, and set things straight so they can keep building.

Other times it's to a soccer match made up of imaginary players. Teams whose names don't exist in the real world but that play a vibrant role in the backyard league we are a part of.

Still other times it's an invitation into the book of the day. To curl up on the couch and read together. To ask questions like "Oh my goodness, what do you think is going to happen now?" or "What do you think it would be like to be a part of this story?"

Whether it's sports or books or blocks, somehow hobbies level the playing field. They can make any consideration of age fly right out the window. Because, at the end of the day, what matters are the things we're all interested in and that help us have fun. And kids know how to have fun. They keep it innocent and pure, and they channel all their creativity and energy and spunk into it, because it's serious business to them. They haven't had a chance to get bogged down by responsibilities or to become in any way jaded by disappointments. Hobbies are just pathways to connection and fun when you're a kid. And since we were all kids at some point, and we all have access to the kid that's still deep within us somewhere, we can let those pathways lead where they're intended to lead . . . to connection and fun.

CHASE THE FUN

What did you love to do as a kid? Is there a way you could use that to connect with the kids in your life sometime soon?

Hobbies Are Fun

Life is more fun if you play games.
ROALD DAHL

- **Writing:** when the perfect combination of words comes together and creates meaning
- **Knitting:** relaxation, stress relief . . . and then a scarf!
- **Juggling:** the joy of zero balls (or flaming batons) dropped
- **Puzzles:** the process of fitting pieces together so the picture is clear and beautiful
- **Gaming:** being transported to a different reality
- **Fishing:** the peace of waiting, the rhythm of casting, and the thrill of the bite
- **Baking:** the birthday boy's smile when he bites into the cupcake you made just for him
- **Tennis:** your brain and your body working together
- **Singing:** when love or ache or sadness or joy takes on a melody and escapes into the atmosphere
- **Hiking:** reaching new heights and breathtaking views
- **Horseback riding:** the strength beneath you, the wind on your face, and the freedom like flying as your horse gallops

- **Gardening:** seeing the first shoots pop through the soil
- **Reading:** visiting new worlds, inhabiting new stories, gaining new perspectives, and never having to leave your couch
- **Playing guitar:** how the right chords in the right order can take you right back to when you first heard that song

Y'all. Look at that list. Even if you don't see your hobby there, doesn't that list sound fun? You know why, right? It's because that list has creativity and connection and brain stimulation and nature and movement and growth and learning and beauty. Whatever brings those things into your life also brings fun.

We NEED fun in our lives. Some of us are fortunate enough to have elements of fun in our jobs and to have fun relationships in our families and with our friends. But there's something a little magic about the fun we CHOOSE to incorporate into our worlds.

That's because it's OURS. It belongs to us. We pick our hobbies because of how they're simultaneously a gift to us AND a gift to the world. Because that's how the broken things get put back together piece by piece, when we're being fully ourselves and making space in all the busyness to protect enjoyment and wonder and whimsy. Hobbies feed our souls and help us feel a few steps closer to Eden.

CHASE THE FUN

Remind yourself of why your hobby is fun.

Hobbies Keep You Humble

Humble yourselves in the presence of the Lord, and He will exalt you.

JAMES 4:10 NASB

don't know about you, but I can be pretty forgetful. It's just that my brain moves fast—really fast—and I can be on to the next idea or thought or plan before I even realize I didn't finish the last one. I need help slowing down and remembering.

I almost feel sheepish saying I need help with that, because sometimes I can convince myself that I should be a little further along on my journey in that area. Kind of a "Get it together, Downs" feeling. It's humbling to need to ask for help. Asking for help is also admitting there's an area of life I just don't have figured out.

But God doesn't ask us to have everything figured out, does He? That's a pressure our culture piles on or that we put on ourselves. He does, however, ask us to be humble.

There's a phrase used in the Bible with some frequency when humility is mentioned: *humble yourself*. There's a choice involved. And an action, right? We get to choose to humble ourselves. And our hobbies are a great place to do that.

Hobbies keep you humble because you're new at them. We need that reminder, don't we? New, inexperienced, novice—these are all good places to be. Wide-open space to learn and grow and discover and create.

It makes me think about how Adam must've felt when God invited him to name the animals in the garden. "Who, me? I've never named animals before. How will I know if I get it right? What if I ruin the possum's reputation for the rest of history because I didn't call him a puff-puff?" I can almost see God's kind smile and hear His voice saying, "Oh, Adam, the pressure's off. You're new at this. I believe you can do it . . . in fact, that's why I asked you. And I'm right here if you need help."

Hobbies keep you humble because they remind you of your limitations. Now, I know that remembering our limitations doesn't sound like that much fun. It's just that there's fun to be discovered on the other side of humbly admitting that I need a break, that I need to participate in something that brings flourishing, and that I can't do it alone. We're not supposed to be great at everything, friends. That's God's job, and He's awesome at it.

CHASE THE FUN

Where do you find humility mixed in with your hobbies?

How to Keep a Hobby a Hobby

For where your treasure is, there your heart will be also.

MATTHEW 6:21

With the rise of the gig economy in recent years, many more people have short-term, freelance, project-based jobs than in the decades when our parents were growing up. Since traditional nine-to-five work isn't as much the norm, society is primed with this really fun openness to making a living in ways that fit your talents and your schedule. But it raises the question: Is this activity you've been doing for fun something you want to turn into a side hustle?

Maybe you've been blogging for a while and what you're writing is resonating with people. Naturally, you'll hear, "When are you going to write a book?" Or when you show friends the stitching that looks exactly like your beloved goldendoodle and that you've had such fun creating, their quick response is, "Oh my goodness, do you sell your work? Could you do one of my mom's dog? She'd love it so much!"

And here's a chance for you to have an honest chat with yourself. It's great to go pro if you want to, if there's demand for what you are uniquely gifted to create. But do you know what's also great? If you decide you want to keep your hobby a hobby. You and I have spent enough time together over the last eighty-eight days that you know I want you to feel all the freedom in the world to simply make space for yourself, for fun, and for leisure activities that you schedule purely for the enjoyment and connection they provide.

And if that's where you are on the matter, I find it helpful to have a bit of a script in my proverbial pocket for when the inevitable question gets asked. It goes something like this: "[Fill-in-the-blank] is a hobby that I just really love doing, and I want to keep it as a way to rest and have fun without having it become a box to check off."

When you keep a hobby a hobby, there's an opportunity for generosity. It's generous to yourself to draw good boundaries that protect and prioritize your fun. And it's generous to others when they want to pay you to make one of your gorgeous cakes for their baby's first birthday party and you get to say, "It's something I just love doing. Why don't you buy the ingredients and let the baking and decorating be my gift?" Goodness gracious, being generous to yourself and to your friends—what's more fun than that?!

CHASE THE FUN

Practice how you'll graciously say no when someone asks if you're going to turn your hobby into a professional endeavor.

When to Go Pro with Your Hobby

Success is not the key to happiness. Happiness is the key to success. If you love what you are doing, you will be successful.

ALBERT SCHWEITZER

You begin a hobby because it's fun. It's life-giving and becomes a regular part of your rhythms. You start out as an amateur and let yourself be clumsy. But over time, you get good at it, whether baking macarons or embroidering initials on sweatshirts or playing piano or golfing. And when you get good at things, you begin to ask yourself, "Could more come of this? Should I make this hobby my side hustle?" Soon others start noticing your extraordinary creations: "Those macarons are beautiful and taste amazing! Can I pay you to make some for a baby shower I'm hosting?" OR "I love your embroidered sweatshirt. Where'd you get it? Oh my word, YOU made it? I'd love to place an order for all the girls in my book club! How much do you charge?"

All this validates what you're learning and how you're growing and how much fun you're having. But if you're trying to decide whether to go pro with your hobby, consider a couple questions:

1. **Do you want to?** If yes, then I encourage you to explore the next step. You don't have to go from hobby to fully formed business plan with five- and ten-year goals and quarterly sales quotas in one fell swoop. Just take a step.

2. **What questions do you have, and who can you ask?** Remind yourself that you're an amateur and that's okay. Ask someone with experience in the field for advice. Offer to pay them for an hour of their time and come prepared with questions. Bonus points if you send them your questions in advance!

Investigating is not committing. Once you have a realistic view of what transitioning your hobby into a side hustle or full-time gig will involve, go back to question 1. And be honest with yourself, because there are costs—financial, sure, but also mental and emotional. If you decide the costs are worth it, muster up your bravery and step forward! If not, that's okay. You still have an awesome hobby to enjoy.

CHASE THE FUN

Daydream about what it would look like
to go pro with one of your hobbies.

Any tips on discovering new fun in new seasons of life? | Kensy

How do I invite people into my fun? | Mary

If I don't find courage to pursue my dreams, will my future self regret it? | Hannah

How do I find fun again when it feels lost in my identity as a mom? | Kristin

What advice would you give to your younger self? | Hilary

How do I discern when it's appropriate to pursue fun to increase joy versus avoiding hard things? | Mikayla

How can I maximize my fun? | Caitlin

How do you find fun in the mundane parts of life? | Samantha

CHASE THE FUN

When You Chase Fun, Joy Follows

The glory of God is man fully alive.

SAINT IRENAEUS

Kids run everywhere. Have you ever noticed that? They don't have to be racing anyone or chasing anyone or in a hurry. They just like to go fast. Kids are also loud, barefoot, upside down, muddy, and giggly all the time . . . sometimes all at the same time. They know what sounds fun to them, and they're unapologetic about doing just that.

We all used to be that way. We all used to think about fun and do what sounded fun, unapologetically. But somewhere along the way, we stopped. (Well, y'all did. YOU grew up and stopped thinking about fun. I didn't! I'm bringing it back!)

Grown-ups stop thinking about fun because things get busy, and we need to be responsible, and life can be stressful.

The serious, churchy word that is semi-more socially acceptable to talk about and is fun-adjacent is *joy*. But how do we find joy? Where do fun and joy meet? Here's what I think: joy is the feeling, and fun is the action.

It's like when you start a car. You have to turn the key. Fun is turning the key. And joy is the car moving forward.

Before you end up with a warm, fragrant, golden loaf of homemade bread, you've got to preheat the oven and knead the dough. Fun is turning the dial to 400 degrees and putting in the risen dough. And joy is how the warmth turns it into delicious bread.

When you chase fun, joy follows. When you do the things that make you smile, that bring you pleasure, and that help you feel peace, the outcome is a baseline of joy.

Now, a lot of times people confuse joy and happiness. They think that having joy means you must always appear upbeat and can never admit to being sad or mad or down. But we know better, don't we? While happiness may be fleeting or circumstantial, joy is that deep-down, unshakable sense that, no matter the circumstances we may face, God is good—really, truly, all-the-way good—and we're going to be okay.

CHASE THE FUN

Do one thing that sounds fun today
and see what joy it sparks.

Fun Requires Vulnerability

> Embracing our vulnerabilities is risky but not nearly as dangerous as giving up on love and belonging and joy—the experiences that make us the most vulnerable. Only when we are brave enough to explore the darkness will we discover the infinite power of our light.
>
> BRENÉ BROWN

You probably wouldn't go to an amusement park on a first date, would you? Sitting next to someone you just met on a roller coaster that is about to spin you upside down and cause you to scream in undignified ways and possibly say words you don't usually say might not be the way to make a winning first impression. It's just too vulnerable a location for the early getting-acquainted phase.

You want to gradually increase the level of vulnerability in a new dating relationship. It's a "use the steps to get into the swimming pool" situation rather than a "diving into the deep end" moment. But you definitely want vulnerability to be a key ingredient at the right time.

It's that way with fun too. Truly having fun, in the purest sense of the word, requires a level of vulnerability. Because fun invites us to try things we've never done before, to be an amateur, to take risks . . . and all of that makes us vulnerable.

If you chase fun and choose to embrace the vulnerability that comes along with it, joy will follow because you are known and loved.

To be loved but not known is so scary, because we're always second-guessing whether someone would leave or reject us "if they only knew . . ." We wonder what will happen when they find out the really tough things we deal with.

To be known but not loved is the deep fear we all face that who we are is just too much or not enough or not good or not worthy.

But to be known AND loved? That's fun. It's fun when we get to give and receive that kind of love because it's a little glimpse of Eden. It's fun when we're vulnerable with each other, because we get to love like God loves. Now, we don't do it perfectly. We have to remember that it's okay to be an amateur at saying "I'm sorry" and "I forgive you" like we learned about on days 19 and 20. But being willing to be vulnerable will lead to the joy AND fun of being known and loved.

CHASE THE FUN

Write down the relationship(s) in which you feel most known and loved. Take a moment to be grateful.

Fun Invites Connection

I make a point to appreciate all the little things in my life.

DOLLY PARTON

When I sat around a dinner table with the team from my publisher after I had just signed the contract to write *That Sounds Fun*, I told them, "If this book hits the *New York Times* bestseller list, we're going to Dollywood!" And . . . spoiler alert . . . it did.

So, we did!

Only, what I had envisioned isn't exactly how things turned out. I was thinking that we'd get my staff team, the publishing team, and some of my friends and family together for a fun-filled day riding rides and eating cinnamon bread at Dollywood. Maybe twenty people, max.

And then I talked about it. To all of my friends. On Instagram and the podcast. And they ALL decided to come. (I mean, not LITERALLY all, but a couple thousand of them. Which was the most fun, and I still haven't gotten over it to the very day that I'm typing these words several months later.)

Want to know one of my very favorite things about that day? Quite a few people bought a ticket, made the trip, and showed up at Dollywood alone. I thought it was so brave. And it made my heart do flips because these individuals knew what I also knew to be true: the friends who were coming to this celebration were safe, warm, fun, welcoming people. They weren't going to let anyone be lonely.

And then I got to watch it happen. By the end of the day when we were doing a meet and greet, I met multiple groups of people who had spent the whole day together gallivanting around Dollywood and having the best time but had never met before that day. I loved it so much. Even better, I still hear from them about how they've stayed in touch with each other. How fun is that?!

I've seen it happen before my very eyes. When you chase fun, joy will follow. Because fun invites connection. And connection tells you you're not alone.

Shared experiences, memories and laughs, inside jokes and stories . . . they all provide this amazing foundation to build friendships and relationships on. And when you build on something that's firm (like joy and connection), what you're creating lasts. It's a way of putting your little corner of the world back together. It's a way of cultivating Eden right here and now.

CHASE THE FUN

Call or text someone with whom you share a fun memory or a great inside joke. Start with, "Remember when we . . .?"

Fun Helps You Remember

He has also set eternity in the human heart.

ECCLESIASTES 3:11

I t's the feeling the second after you stop laughing until your stomach aches and you have tears streaming down your face. When you catch your breath and almost can't even think of what was so funny in the first place.

It's the take-your-breath-away moment when you crest the last hill on your hike and reach the point where the valley opens up beneath you and stretches out for miles before you and looks exactly like you imagine heaven will.

It's when you look around the table at your dinner club or around the patio during a particularly rousing discussion about the novel you just read for book club, and you want to take a snapshot in your mind because you wish the moment would never end.

It's when you're in the middle of doing something fun and you say, "This is just like when my grandmother and I used to . . ." or "I haven't had this much fun since I was a kid."

It's when we just don't have the words to describe the feeling we're having. Fun helps us remember the simple and pure times in our lives. The peace of when things were less complicated and weighty.

And, as strange as it sounds, fun even helps us remember a time we haven't yet experienced but that we all yearn for.

See, the Old Testament book of Ecclesiastes tells us that God put eternity in our hearts. He built it into us. The longing for Eden . . . the paradise of being fully *known*, fully *loved*, and fully *with* Him.

Sometimes when we're having fun, we're experiencing eternity. A taste of what will one day never end. When you chase fun and you remember, joy will follow, because someday that thing you hope never ends will actually never end.

Fun tells us about forever.

CHASE THE FUN

Think about the last time you had an "I wish this would never end" experience. What was it that made it feel that way?

Where Faith Meets Fun

Do not grieve, for the joy of the LORD is your strength.

NEHEMIAH 8:10

f joy is the emotion and fun is the action that gets us there, what the combination of joy and fun builds in us is strength. It's not the most logical or obvious conclusion people jump to when they think about fun, but it's right there in the Bible. The joy of the Lord is our strength.

That verse from the book of Nehemiah appears as part of a sermon being shared with the small-ish group of God's people who have returned from exile to rebuild the wall around Jerusalem. They're heartbroken over their city and over their sin, but the preacher encourages them to find joy because they belong to God. This whole moment is a kind of crescendo of the restoration that the Lord is bringing about in their story and in their city.

God is about restoration. And He wants to restore you. He wants to put together pieces of your heart that have broken apart because of poor decisions you made or others made that have affected you in hurtful ways. He wants a restored you to help restore those around you, the people He's specifically placed in your sphere of influence and entrusted to you. He wants to restore your church and your neighborhood and your school and your city.

God is about restoration. Eden was His idea, and then He imprinted it in our hearts and gave us a longing for the restoration and flourishing that come from knowing Him and the joy He provides.

Living a life that seeks restoration makes us strong so that we can carry joy and hope everywhere we go. And with our eyes and hearts open, we can see how God has restored in the past, which builds our faith in the now, so that the way we look toward the future is entirely covered with joyful hope.

Chase the Fun

Write down ways you have seen God restore your heart, your relationships, your circumstances.

Invite Others into Your Fun

We were together. I forget the rest.
WALT WHITMAN

Some days go precisely the way they're planned. All the boxes get checked and all the lines are charting up and to the right.

Some days go exactly opposite of the way you're hoping. Like lightning striking when you're already up to your knees in a puddle and your house is on fire.

But most days are somewhere in between, aren't they? Some things go great, others are tough, and most are just fine, but nothing dramatically special. The magic of fun is how it brightens up and boosts those normal, mundane days.

Once, at the end of a day that hadn't quite gone the way I'd hoped it would but that still had some magic in it, my friend David said, "Most anything CAN be fun. It just depends on us."

And I said, "Yes. I want to get THAT as a tattoo."

Most anything can be fun. It just depends on us.

Not just me and not just you. It depends on us. I think that may be the secret sauce here. Eden wasn't complete with just Adam. Before the snake, before sin, before anything went wrong, it was already wrong for Adam to be alone.

Fun is more fun when we're not alone in it.

Life is just better with than without.

And all it requires from us is to extend the invitation. Look up once in a while and ask yourself who's missing. Who would enjoy this game? What if we expand the dinner club so two more friends can be a part? Who have I not hiked with in a while? The worst they could do is say no. But let me tell you a little secret: people rarely say no to fun they're personally invited into. It's too sacred. It may take a couple of scheduling attempts because calendars are crazy, y'all, but stick with it.

We all want connection, and it's a gift we can all give.

CHASE THE FUN

Call or text or email or DM a friend
about getting together soon.

Share Your Fun

> When you have once seen the glow of happiness on the face of a beloved person, you know that a man can have no vocation but to awaken that light on the faces surrounding him.
>
> ALBERT CAMUS

You are a leader. You may argue with me about this, but the fun thing about being the author of this little devotional is that even if you argue, I just can't hear it. You've got my words for you, but I can't hear you if you're yelling back at me! But I know it's true, so even if you want to push back, just hear me out. You're a leader. You have influence in someone's life. If you have one follower on Instagram, if you have birthed or adopted or fostered or taught or loved or coached a child, if you have led a small group, if you do volunteer work, if you manage a team, if you have a friend . . . you are a leader.

Someone's watching, paying attention, and learning from you. The choices you make have these ripple effects in the world. And one of the ripples you get to make is sharing your fun.

What happens when you share your fun?

You remind other people that fun matters. Sometimes all it takes for a friend to take a step toward the fun, rest, and joy they desperately need is the simple reminder that it matters. That they deserve to have time and space built into their lives that will help them flourish in that way. And a lot of times, we can hear that and receive it better from someone else than we can from ourselves.

You inspire new ideas. When you share your fun, you may be sharing something that feels obvious to you, but it's the first time someone who follows you has thought of it that way. You plant seeds that take root and grow.

You invite connections. One of the best ways to share your fun is by inviting others into it. Is there a game, activity, or pastime that you find especially fun? When you ask someone else to join in, you create connection. Maybe they don't decide that it's a hobby they're going to stick with. But who knows, maybe you just found your new championship doubles partner!

CHASE THE FUN

Share your fun today. Post online about what sounds fun to you.

Don't Judge Your Own Fun

> Make a careful exploration of who you are and the work you have been given, and then sink yourself into that. Don't be impressed with yourself. Don't compare yourself with others. Each of you must take responsibility for doing the creative best you can with your own life.
>
> GALATIANS 6:4-5 MSG

There's a difference between judgment and judging.

Not long ago, my friend who is a really talented photographer shared with me about her process for editing the photos she takes. It was fascinating to me. There are all these tiny judgments that she makes to decide how she wants to curate the look and the final product that she's going for. Saturation and exposure and some other technical terms I didn't exactly know but could piece together the general idea. Her judgment is part of what makes her brilliant at photography and what makes it so fun for her.

What she's not doing in those moments is judging her work. She's not saying to herself, "This is bad. I've got to change it." And she's definitely not saying, "I'm a terrible photographer because this photo needs to be edited." Do you see the difference?

You get to use your judgment to make decisions about how you spend your free time. And I encourage you to use your judgment wisely. But as your friend and Fun Coach (I like the title more every time I use it!), I really must protest if you are judging your fun.

You get to like what you like. You get to enjoy what you enjoy. You don't have to defend it or compare it. You get to do your creative best with what you've got!

And when you do, it gets at the heart of the question "What brings flourishing in my life and the lives of the people I love?" Because that's the goal here. To find what makes your heart flourish. It may feel like hard work and smell like long days and sometimes make you cry or throw your phone. But if your heart flourishes, if the enemy is silenced from telling you that your life doesn't matter, you know that even the tiniest steps toward something your gut says you were made to do are worth it.

CHASE THE FUN

Look at yourself in the mirror and say out loud, "I get to like what I like. What I am made to do matters." Do it again if that helps you believe and remember it.

Don't Judge Someone Else's Fun

> If you judge people, you have no time to love them.
>
> MOTHER TERESA

There's a thing that happens among a lot of my friends in the autumn of the year. Somehow it seems to happen both gradually and all at once. When the very first hint of cool, crisp mornings comes on the scene or even one leaf begins its metamorphosis from green to orange, it starts: the emergence of the pumpkin spice latte into the ecosystem of my social media world. Now, you know me—I'm a chai girl, so I am all-inclusive when it comes to spicy, warm, creamy drinks!

The thing that also seems to arrive in the very next breath is outcry from others, seemingly made bitter and grumpy from all the summer heat, who find pumpkin-flavored beverages detestable. They complain about how basic it is to become excited about a seasonal drink, and then they pile on stereotypes about scarves and boots and oversized sweaters. Rude.

I point this out because I don't necessarily think that your choice of spices in your latte has much to do with fun (although maybe in some small way it does?), but I DO think our culture has gotten a little opinion-happy with how quickly we are willing to criticize or judge what other people enjoy.

And here's what I want to say to that: there's room for everyone. When it comes to fun, there's so much space for people to have different preferences and different likes and different interests. Another person enjoying something that you don't has no bearing on the value and worth of what you like. It just doesn't. There's room for everyone.

So, like what you like. And celebrate everyone else's right to like what they like. It's just better that way. When you celebrate what someone else likes, you may even open yourself up to a new discovery, to something that hadn't occurred to you before but that you actually really enjoy. Why limit the possibilities for fun by judging it?

CHASE THE FUN

Ask someone a question about what they enjoy. Listen to their answer and maybe even ask a follow-up question!

What Sounds Fun to You?

> It is not in doing what you like, but in liking what you do that
> is the secret of happiness.
>
> J. M. BARRIE

There are a couple of things I know about you here on day 100. You're the kind of person who starts a thing and finishes it. You are determined and you are curious and you are FUN. You're taking steps toward being the person you want to be, and I think that's remarkable.

When you chase fun, joy follows. And joy makes you strong. And strength gives you courage to be fully YOU in the world. You showing up fully you is just the kind of flourishing that the Lord intended in Eden. It's heaven come to earth.

And when you share it with others, you invite them into that same journey. So that's my next fun challenge to you: think about who you want to encourage to read *Chase the Fun* too. Post about it, use it as your next small group or book club read. Since technology makes the world smaller but our platforms bigger, use that to inspire others to start their own chase. Because we all need to discover or rediscover the joys of being an amateur, the power of falling in love, and why hobbies matter.

Doing anything for one hundred days will change you. You are different from when you first picked up this book, and my guess is it isn't just about fun. I hope you've done some of the self-exploration and purposeful remembering and deep connecting that fun can make way for.

Because we have chased the fun together. We are chasing the fun. And what sounds fun to you matters. Go for it, friend.

CHASE THE FUN

Snap a photo of the cover of this book and of yourself doing something fun. Don't forget to tag me @anniefdowns with the hashtag #ChaseTheFunBook!

ACKNOWLEDGMENTS

The longer I write books, the more I learn that this isn't a solo sport. It took so many people giving their very best in their area of expertise for you to have this book in your hands today. I'm deeply grateful.

Thank you to my coworkers at Downs Books Inc. and That Sounds Fun Network for giving so much of yourself to the work we get to do. Work hard. Pray hard. Rest hard. Play hard.

KCH Entertainment, I'm so grateful for how y'all invest in all parts of what we do. I feel so lucky that y'all care so deeply about me and our work.

Ashley Warren, thank you for putting your hands and heart in this devotional along with me. Andrea Doering and Amy Nemecek, thank you for taking the best we had to offer and making it better.

Lisa Jackson, thank you for standing beside me in this expression of my work and creativity and heart. I'm glad we're doing this for a long time. And thank you to the whole team at Revell—we're having more fun than we deserve.

Thank you to my friends and family and miniBFFs for being such joy in my life. I can write alone because I spend my life with you.

To you, my reader friend, I am beyond grateful that whether you got here from past books, tour stops, podcast episodes, or social media posts, your friendship allows me to keep doing this writing thing that I love so deeply. From the bottom of my heart, thank you.

To Jesus, You saved me once, but You rescue me all the time. This season of writing has been one for this book, but also ONE FOR THE BOOKS, and Your constant friendship has been air to my lungs and hope to my heart. I hope I'm known for chasing fun and teaching others how to do the same, but I mostly hope I'm known for chasing You.

Annie F. Downs is a bestselling author, sought-after speaker, and successful podcast host based in Nashville, Tennessee. Engaging and honest, she makes readers and listeners alike feel as if they've been longtime friends. Founder of the That Sounds Fun Network—which includes her aptly named flagship show, *That Sounds Fun*—and author of multiple bestselling books like *100 Days to Brave* and *Remember God*, Annie shoots straight and doesn't shy away from the tough topics. But she always finds her way back to the truth that God is good and that life is a gift. Annie is a huge fan of laughing with friends, confetti, soccer, and boiled peanuts (preferably from a backroads Georgia gas station).

Read more at **anniefdowns.com** and find her (embarrassingly easily) all over the internet **@anniefdowns**.

Loved this book?

Keep finding the fun with bestselling author
Annie F. Downs!

Adults and children will see how fun can
be had in every place, at any time.